Relationship with God

Felicia Diane Williams

ISBN 978-1-0980-7873-7 (paperback)
ISBN 978-1-0980-7874-4 (digital)

Christian Faith Publishing, Inc.
832 Park Avenue
Meadville, PA 16335
www.christianfaithpublishing.com

Printed in the United States of America

Chapter 1

I remember it like it was yesterday. My mom and I were sitting in a church at someone's funeral in Dallas, Texas. I was eight years old. My mom was explaining to me about when she dies, this is how it will be; only she would be the person lying in the coffin. She went on to say when she dies, people will come from all over the world to say their last good-byes to her. We talked about how people will be standing in the front of the church telling everyone how they feel about her. She also said some people may even be crying because they will miss her. Then she said, "Stand up, Tammy. It's time to view the body."

She grabbed my hand, and we proceeded to walk around the church. We glanced at the body and walked out of the church to our car. Once we got in the car, she said the coffin will be closed when she dies.

I said, "Then I won't be able to say good-bye to you." She said I will be able to tell her good-bye while she's living. I said, "I never want to tell you good-bye, and can we please stop talking about this?" My mom said we got one more place to go and we will go home and not talk about it anymore. When the cars started lining up, my mom got in line with the other cars.

My mom said, "All the cars are lining up because they are taking the person in the coffin to the cemetery to bury them."

I said, "Are they going to do you like that?" She said yes. She started talking again about what's going to happen when she dies. I asked her, "Why are we still talking about this? You don't want me anymore."

My mom said, "I love you, Tammy, and I want you forever. I just want you to know if you wake up one day and I'm not here and someone tells you I'm gone to be with God, it only means you won't be able to see me physically anymore, but I will always be in your heart."

So I said, "If you're dead, how can you be in my heart?"

She said, "It's hard for you to understand right now, but you will one day. Just know Mommy loves you with all her heart and soul."

And I told her, "I love you with all my heart and soul." Well, we finally made it to the cemetery. We parked and got out of the car and started walking to the grave site. I started crying, and my mom said, "What's wrong, Tammy?" I couldn't say anything. I couldn't stop crying. My mom grabbed me and hugged me real tight, and then we headed back to the car. Once we were in the car, she said, "Baby, it's okay to cry, but Mommy doesn't want you to cry at my funeral. It's not a sad thing when people die. It's a celebration.

"I want you to be strong and happy, be my big girl that I've taught you to be, and keep praying to God like I taught you, because God will always protect you no matter what, and he will never leave you no matter what the situation is."

I was my mom's praying child. We prayed every day and any time of the day. We finally made it home, and my dad was there. I wasn't happy to see him because he was always fussing at my mom and being very violent to her. Eventually she left him. I loved him. I just didn't like the way he treated my mom. We moved out of the house into an apartment. My mom seemed to be very happy, and I was very happy too, because my dad couldn't hurt her anymore. Once we got settled in our place, my dad would come around and visit. He had stopped fussing and hitting my mom. Every time he came, he would bring me candies, toys, and clothes. After living there for a while, this lady came over to visit us. She had her husband and two kids with her. The lady kept saying, "Come give me a hug, Tammy." I didn't go near her because I didn't know who she was. My mom made me hug her. Then everyone sat down. I sat down beside my mom.

My mom said, "This lady is your real mom."

I said, "What are you talking about? You're my mom."

She repeated it again. So I asked her, "Do you not want me?"

My mom said, "I love you, Tammy, with all my heart and soul. If something should happen to me, you will have to go live with her." I got up and went in my room and lay on the bed and started crying. My mom came in my room and sat on the bed and said they had left. I was glad to hear that. I got up and started hugging my mom, then she said, "Let's get down on our knees and pray." I put my elbows on the bed and put my hands together and started saying the Lord's Prayer with my mom.

"Our Father who art in heaven, hallowed be thy name. Thy kingdom come. Thy will be done on earth as it is in heaven. Give us this day our daily bread and forgive us our trespasses as we forgive those who trespass against us, and lead us not into temptations but deliver us from evil. Amen." I don't understand the Lord's Prayer all the way, but my mom says as I get older, I will learn to understand.

Chapter 2

Some months passed, and my mom sent me to live with my aunt while she went on vacation. My mom had started going on vacation a lot more than she used to. I didn't mind staying with my aunt Tina. She was a lot of fun, plus she had a son my age, and we always had a lot of fun too. Normally when my mom went on vacation, she didn't stay away that long, but this time it seemed like forever. One day I asked my aunt, "When is my mom coming back from vacation?" She said soon. When my mom went on vacation, we had just got out of school for the summer, and now it's almost time for school to start back. My mom had never stayed on vacation this long. Well, one day my cousin and I were playing in this graveyard across the street from the apartments they lived in. We mostly played tag and hide behind the tombstones. I was chasing my cousin, and he fell in one of the empty plots.

I tried to reach him to help him get out, but I couldn't because my arms weren't long enough. He started crying, and I did too. I told him, "I will be back. I'm going to get your mom." I told my aunt Tina what happened, and we both ran to the graveyard to help my cousin. When we made it there, some man was pulling my cousin out of the grave plot. My cousin was still crying, and I started crying again because I was so happy to see him.

The man said, "Do not come back to that graveyard anymore."

My aunt told him, "Thank you for helping my son, and don't worry, they won't be back." We told him thank you too. And we walked back to the apartment.

My aunt put us on punishment. She said we couldn't go outside and play until she decided when she was taking us off punishment. We didn't care because we had just as much fun inside. Later that day, my aunt received a phone call from my mom. She told my aunt Tina to bring me home. I was so excited. I couldn't wait to see her. When we arrived there, the door was open. I walked in, and the first person I saw was the woman who my mom said was my real mom. Her husband and kids were there too.

My mom called out to me. She said, "Come in my room." I ran in there and leaped on the bed and started hugging and kissing her. She held me in her arms for a long time. I told her I missed her so much. I asked if I could sleep with her that night. She didn't give me an answer. I knew something was wrong because she had lost so much weight, but she had a beautiful smile on her face.

My mom said, "You remember when I took you to that funeral?" I said yes. She said, "Tammy, now is the time for me to go be with God." I broke down and started crying.

I asked her, "Please don't leave me." She said she didn't have a choice. I said, "Take me with you."

She said, "It doesn't work like that." Then she said, "It's time for you to go live with your real mom."

I told her, "I don't want to go with her." I begged her to let me stay with her, but she continued to tell me no. She told me to stop crying and be her big girl. I wrapped my arms around her and asked her, "Please don't leave me."

She said, "I will never leave you. I will always be in your heart, and I love you with all my heart and soul."

I said, "I love you with all my heart and soul too."

She said the name of the lady in the living room was Janice, and she really was my real mom, and it's time to live with her now. My mom said, "She will love you and take care of you like I have."

My mom's name was Doris, and I knew no one will ever love me better than her. I love my mom so much. I wanted to die too so I could be with her. Then Janice walked in the room and said it's time to go. I hugged my mom again with tears running down my face. I knew that was going to be the last time I saw her. My mom told

Janice my bags were already packed and that the suitcases were in my room. I asked my mom one more time to let me stay with her. She said, "No, you're going to Denver, Colorado, to live with your birth mother."

My mother had accumulated a lot of trophies from playing card games. I asked my mom if I could have one of her trophies. She said, "Yes, baby, get one."

Janice's husband said, "We got to go. I've got to be at work by Monday." Janice's husband was a scary-looking big tall man. Tears continued to run down my face. I said my last good-bye to my mom and left with my new family. As we proceeded to their car, I began to silently pray to God. I asked God to please protect me from the strangers I was leaving with. My mom told me anytime I was scared, I should pray to God because he will always protect me. I asked God to protect and watch over my mom while I was away. My heart hurt so bad. I felt like my mom sent me away because she didn't want me anymore. My mom also taught me to thank God every day, even when things are not going my way, because he is the only one who knows what's best for me. Right now I'm not understanding any of this. As we entered the car, Janice's husband told me to sit behind the driver's seat, so I did. Tears were still rolling down my face. Her husband pulled in a gas station and sent Janice in the store to pay for the gas.

Once Janice got in the store, her husband said to me, "Wipe them goddam tears up, and all that damn crying stops right now, and if you don't stop, I'm going to take my belt off and beat the hell out of you." My heart started beating really fast. I wiped my face with my shirt, but I couldn't control my tears. Janice got back in the car. She looked at me and said it's going to be all right. I didn't say anything. I started looking out of the window and started to say the Lord's Prayer silently.

Well, Janice had two kids: a son named Benny Jr. and a daughter named Belinda.

Belinda started talking to me. She said, "Don't cry. My mom told me you're my big sister, and we are going to take care of you now." I said okay. That made me feel a little better. Every time I would look straight ahead, I could see Janice's husband looking at me through the rearview mirror, and that would make my heart beat so fast. It was a scary feeling. So I would try not to look in that direction. It seemed like we had been driving forever. I wasn't sure where we were going. I just knew it was a long ways from my home.

Chapter 3

Finally we pulled into their driveway. Upon entering their garage, Janice said, "Home sweet home. Tammy, this is your new home now." Janice's husband started taking the suitcases out of the car. Janice said, "Grab your suitcase, Tammy, and follow me." As we entered the house, the phone was ringing. Janice went to answer the phone, and I followed her. While she was on the phone, she started crying. Janice told whoever was on the phone, "I'll call you back. I've got to talk to Tammy." Then Janice said, "Come here, Tammy. Let's go in the living room and sit down."

While sitting there, Janice said to me, "Your mom just died." I just looked at Janice. I didn't say anything. I couldn't cry. She tried to put her arms around me, but I was scared of her and her husband. I just sat there on the couch. Janice's husband came in the living room. He saw the tears on Janice's face and asked her what's wrong. She said, "Doris just died." Janice said, "Put the luggage back in the car. We are going back to Dallas."

Janice's husband looked at me and said, "I'm sorry your mom died, but we are not going back to Dallas for the funeral." I didn't say anything. I just sat there.

Janice said, "Yes, we are. Even if I have to drive by myself, we are going."

Her husband said, "Let's go in our room and discuss this."

Janice said, "Tammy, come with me. I'm going to show you your room." I followed her. Janice said, "Make yourself comfortable, and I will be back to check on you." I went and got my suitcases from the living room and took out the trophy my mom gave me. I lay on the bed and laid my mom's trophy on my chest. I thought about that funeral my mom took me to, and I realized she really wanted me, but it really was her time to be with God. Then the tears started pouring down my face.

I missed my mom so much. I started praying to God, and I said, "I don't have to ask you to take care of my mom anymore because she's safe with you, but I really need you right now. I'm all alone and don't know what to do." I said the Lord's Prayer, and I just lay there on the bed and thought about my mom. It seemed like I could hear her sweet voice saying, "Tammy, be my big girl like I taught you to be."

I must have fallen asleep because Janice's husband woke me up and said, "Come in the kitchen and eat dinner." I told him I wasn't hungry. He said, "Get your ass up and go to the table and eat your dinner."

I got up and sat down at the table. I wasn't eating. I just sat there. Janice's husband said, "Tammy, you better eat that shit because we don't waste food around here." I still didn't eat. Janice's husband said, "I guess you will be sitting here all night, because you're going to eat that food."

Janice said, "Drink your juice, and you can go back to your room," so I did and lay back down on the bed. I started wondering, *Where is my dad, and does he know where I'm at? I don't think he knows because he wouldn't let anyone take me away. My daddy loves me. As soon as he finds out where I'm at, he's going to come get me.*

I fell asleep while I was thinking about my parents. The next morning, Janice woke me up and told me to go take a shower, get dressed, and come eat breakfast. I told her I wasn't hungry. Janice said I needed to eat to stay strong. So I ate some cereal and went in the den and started watching cartoons with her kids. Janice came in the den and said we weren't going back to Dallas right away, but we were going back for the funeral.

I asked Janice, "Does my dad know I'm here with you?"

She said, "Yes, and you will see him at the funeral." I was glad to hear that because when he sees me, I know he's going to keep me with him.

11

After Janice left, I continued watching TV while playing dolls with Belinda, and I was tickling Benny Jr., then Janice's husband came in the den and sat down. I got up and went to my room, which was next to the den, and closed the door. Janice's husband came in my room and said, "We don't close doors around here unless it's the bathroom door or I give you permission to close the door, and right now, this door stays open unless I tell you something different," and he left my room.

After he left, I started praying to God for protection from Janice's husband. *I'm scared of him, God. I think he wants to hurt me. I don't think he likes me being here. Please, God, when I see my daddy, please give me to him. I don't want to be here. My mom told me you have control of everything.*

Janice's husband came back in my room and said, "Stop all that damn whining. This is your home now. I don't want to see no more tears, and you will do as I say or I will beat the hell out of you." Then he said, "From now on, when I say something to you, open your mouth up and answer. My name is Benny, and that is what you will call me." Then he said, "Follow me." He took me to their laundry room where an ironing board was set up. He asked me, "Do you know how to iron?" I shook my head left to right, expressing no because I was scared to talk to him. Benny said, "What did I tell you about that shit?"

So I said, "No, Benny. I don't know." Benny plugged the iron up and showed me where to set the heating switch. I paid close attention to what he was doing. The whole time my heart was beating so fast. He laid his pants on the ironing board and showed me how to iron his pants.

Benny asked me, "Do you understand?" I said yes. He said, "Don't fuck up my pants," and he walked out of the room. His pants were bigger than the ironing board and bigger than me. I was not understanding why he wanted me to do this. I'd never ironed before. My mom did all the ironing. I was afraid Benny would beat me, so I did the best I could. It seemed like I was struggling for hours ironing Benny's pants. Benny came back and snatched his pants off the ironing board and said, "Tammy, you fucked up my pants," and started back showing me again how he wanted his pants ironed. Janice came in the room and told me to go in the kitchen and eat. I was scared to move. I looked up at Benny.

Benny said, "You can go eat, but you will learn how to iron my clothes." So I went to the kitchen to eat.

Janice said, "When you're done eating, do the dishes," and left the kitchen. After I ate, I sat there. I had never done dishes before. I didn't know where to start first.

Benny came in the kitchen to put his plate in the sink. He said to me, "Why are you not washing those dishes?" I didn't say anything. He said, "Get your ass up."

Then Janice came in the room and asked me, "Have you ever washed dishes before?" I said no. So Janice said, "Come on, I will show you," and she did.

After we were done, I took a bath and went to bed. While lying in bed, I started talking to God. I asked, "God, please protect me from Benny. He's always talking about beating me, and now that my mom is with you, could you please tell her I love her with all my heart and soul? Please tell her I miss her so much." Then I said the Lord's Prayer and fell asleep.

Chapter 4

A few days passed by, and one morning, Janice woke me up and said, "Pack your bags. We are leaving this morning to go back to Dallas for your mom's funeral."

All I had to do was get ready because I never unpacked my suitcase. I only got out what I needed to wear for the days we were in Colorado. Whenever Janice would wash my clothes, I would put them back in my suitcase so when we make it back to Dallas, I will be living with my daddy. Janice's husband decided he would drive us back to Dallas so she wouldn't have to drive alone. When we got in the car, I sat behind Janice.

Benny said to me, "What the hell do you think you're doing?" I didn't say anything because I didn't know what he was talking about. Janice's husband said, "Slide your ass behind me. Every time we get in the car, you sit behind me, and I don't want to tell you that again."

I didn't understand why it was so important to sit behind him, but I moved over and sat behind him. I immediately started talking to God silently. I asked God, *When we get to Dallas, will you please find my daddy so I can live with him? I'm scared of these people.* Then I just looked out of my window. I was too afraid to look forward. We drove all day. By the time we made it to Dallas, it was dark. Janice and her husband decided to stay in a hotel for the night.

They got two rooms. There was a door between the rooms so we could go in each other's room without going outside. I didn't talk to Janice or her husband unless they said something to me. I stayed in my room, and all I could think about was my mom. I missed her so much. Tears started running down my face. Janice's daughter,

Belinda, went and told her mom I was crying. Janice came in the room and sat beside me on the bed. She asked me how I was feeling. I didn't respond. She said my mom's funeral was tomorrow, and she's going to explain to me how things will be at the funeral.

Before I could tell her my mom had already discussed this with me, her husband came in the room and said, "Leave her alone. She's fine. Stop treating her like a baby." And he said, "Tammy, what did I tell you about that damn crying?"

Janice said, "Leave her alone." He husband told her to take her ass back in the room, and he followed her. I lay back across the bed and tried real hard not to cry anymore. I started thinking about my mom again. She always had a smile on her face. She would give me hugs and kisses all the time, and she would smell so good.

I wanted to get on my knees and say the Lord's Prayer before I went to sleep, but I was too scared to move. So I asked God to forgive me for not praying on my knees, and then I said the Lord's Prayer silently. I wanted to get up and get my mom's trophy and hold it while I sleep, but my bag was in the room with Janice. I wasn't going in there, so I fell asleep thinking about my mom. The next day came. We got ready to go to the funeral. As I entered the car, I almost forgot I had to sit behind Janice's husband. I entered the car on Janice's side, but I moved over before he got in the car.

As we drove to the funeral, I thought about what my mom said. She said when people die, it isn't a bad thing. It's a celebration. You're going to be with the Lord. I was not sure how I was supposed to feel about that, but I really missed my mom, and I was going to be her big girl and try not to cry. As we entered the church, I was looking for my daddy. Then this lady came up to me and grabbed my hand and took me to the front of the church and sat me beside my daddy. I was so happy to see my daddy and very sad to see my mom in a coffin. I just grabbed hold of my daddy and cried.

I know my mom said when people die, it's a celebration, but I was not feeling the celebration at that moment. All I wanted to do was leave and go to my daddy's house. There were a lot of people talking and singing at my mom's funeral. I sat there thinking about my mom and trying real hard not to cry, because I know she wanted me to be her big girl. Then all of a sudden they opened the casket. My daddy grabbed my hand, and we walked up to the casket, and I started screaming and crying. My daddy picked me up and took me outside, and then we got into this limousine. I asked my dad if I was going to live with him now. Before he could give me an answer, my aunt Tina, her son Randy, my aunt Grace, and my two uncles, Joe and Mark, got in the car. Everyone was hugging and kissing me. I was very happy to see them.

My cousin Randy sat down beside me and asked me, "Where have you been?" I told him my mom sent me to stay with this lady named Janice and her family. Randy said, "Why are you not staying with your dad?" When I got ready to ask my daddy if I was going to live with him now, the car door opened, and everyone started getting out of the car. I asked my daddy if Randy and I could stay in the car.

My daddy said no and told us to get out of the car, and we did. As we approached the grave site, I saw Janice and her family sitting down under a tent. We sat down in front of them. After my mom was laid to rest, my daddy told Janice to meet us at his house. When we got back in the limousine, it was only me and him, so I asked him if I was going to be living with him now. My daddy said, "Wait till we get to my house, and I will explain everything to you." In my mind, I knew my daddy was going to keep me because he loved me.

When we arrived at his house, he asked me if I was hungry or wanted something to drink. I said I wasn't hungry, but I would like something to drink. My dad gave me a Sprite and sat down beside me and said, "Do you understand why your mom died?" I said no. My daddy said my mom died of cancer.

I asked him, "What does that mean?"

He said, "It's a disease that when people get that, it eats away their body to a point they can't live anymore like me and you." I asked my dad why the doctors couldn't save her. He said, "It's a disease that there's no cure for it. Don't worry about her. She's gone to a better place now." Then he said, "Do you understand?" I said no, and my daddy said, "You will one day." Then I asked him if I can live with him now. He said no, because he worked all the time and had no one to keep me.

I said, "Can I stay with Aunt Tina?"

He said no. Then my daddy said, "Janice is my sister, and she's your real mother."

I told my dad, "I don't understand," so he started telling me this story. He said he and his wife (my mom) lived in Dallas, Texas, and Janice lived in a small town called Jefferson, Texas. And he came down from Dallas to visit her and other family members.

When he went to her house, she wasn't home. He said he wasn't surprised because Janice liked to go to clubs and party. So he went on to visit his cousin Mike. When he arrived there, Mike was sitting in his yard. When my daddy approached him, Mike said, "Did you know your sister went to jail last night for fighting in the club?"

My daddy said, "No. Is she still in jail?"

Mike said, "Yes, if no one has bailed her out." My daddy left and went to the police station to check on Janice, and true enough, she was still in jail, so he bailed her out.

After he bailed her out, my daddy asked her, "Where is Tammy?" Janice said she had been drinking, and she couldn't remember who she left me with. My daddy said I was around one year old, and they started going to his family's and friends' houses looking for me, and they weren't having any luck finding me. They pulled into a service station to gas up. My daddy said his cousin Dorothy approached him while pumping gas and asked him if he had seen Janice because she left her baby with her. My daddy asked her where I was. She said in the back seat of her car. My daddy told her Janice was in the car, so Dorothy got Janice, and she went and got me out of the car. My daddy said he asked Janice if he could take me home to his wife. She couldn't have kids because she had cancer. Janice agreed to let my daddy have me for now or until Doris got too sick to keep me. My daddy said my mom got stronger when she got me. She lived longer than the doctor expected.

Then my daddy said, "I'm your uncle Ray, not your daddy, your real mom's brother." I asked him again to please let me stay with him. He said, "No, it's time for you to live with Janice."

I told my daddy I was scared of Janice and her husband. My daddy said, "They won't hurt you when you get used to them. You will be all right, and you got to get used to calling me Uncle Ray." It wasn't long after that conversation that Janice and her family walked in. Janice asked my daddy, I mean Uncle Ray, if he had explained the situation, why I had to live with her. My uncle Ray said yes, and Janice told me to call her Mama, and her husband's name was Benny. I didn't say anything. I just sat there.

Then Benny said, "It's time to go home now." He needed to go back to work. I hugged my daddy and left with Janice and her family. When I got in the car, I sat on the passenger's side behind Janice. In my mind, I was thinking, *My mom is gone, my daddy is not my daddy, and I'm all alone with these strange people.* I looked out of the window, and in my mind, I started talking to God. *God, all I have is you now. I don't have anyone else to love me, and can you please protect me from these people?* I went on to say the Lord's Prayer. After that, I just looked out of the window as we continued home.

Chapter 5

After Benny drove for a while, he pulled into Dairy Queen to get everyone something to eat. Janice took us to the bathroom and told us to go sit down with Benny to eat while she used the bathroom and changed Benny Jr. So we sat down and started eating.

Benny said to me, "Tammy, when you get back in the car, sit your ass behind me. I'm not going to keep telling you." He scared me every time he said something to me, so I stopped eating. Then he said I better eat up all my food because we don't waste food. Janice came out of the bathroom and told Benny to quit fussing at me.

Benny stopped fussing at me and told everyone to eat up so we can get back on the road. This time when I sat in the car, I sat behind Benny so I wouldn't get fussed at. Every time I looked forward, Benny would be looking at me through his rearview mirror, so I would only look out of my window and start talking to God silently in my mind. I said to God, *Please protect me from Benny. I feel he wants to hurt me.* And then I told God, *I miss my mom so much, and can you please tell her I'm trying really hard to be her big girl? But I'm so scared right now of these people you left me with.* I didn't know what else to say to God, so I said the Lord's Prayer and fell asleep.

The next thing I knew, Janice was waking me up. She said, "Get up, Tammy. We are at home. Get your suitcase and go in your room and finish sleeping." So I did. Before I went back to sleep, I started talking to God. I said, *God, I still don't understand the whole situation. I miss my daddy. My daddy, I mean Uncle Ray, could have kept me if he really wanted me. God, I need you to protect me from Benny. I'm so scared of him.* Then I fell asleep thinking about my mom.

The next morning, I woke up, and Benny was in my room standing by the door. I guess he was watching me sleep. My heart started beating really fast. Benny said it's time to get up and go take a shower and get ready for breakfast. I didn't get up until he left my room; he scared me so bad. After I got ready and ate breakfast, Janice said, "We are going shopping today to get you some school clothes." I was going to the third grade. Normally I would be excited about going back to school. My mom would take me shopping for new clothes. But this time I was not excited about anything. I just missed my mom.

I thought it would be Janice and her kids going, but Benny went too. When we got to the store, Benny and Janice started picking out clothes for me. I liked everything Janice picked but I couldn't get them because Benny didn't like them. After Benny picked out my clothes, he told me to try them on and come out and let him see how they looked on me. The tops were okay, but the pants were too tight. Benny said the clothes looked good on me. I asked Janice if she can get me a bigger size for my pants. Before Janice could answer, Benny said, "Hell no. Those pants fit her perfect."

Janice said okay, then Benny told Janice to go pick me some panties and socks out. Her kids stayed with Benny, and Janice and I were alone, so I asked her if she could please get me some bigger-size pants. She said no and stop complaining. I didn't say anything else the rest of the day. Benny paid for the clothes, and we left and went to a shoe store. Benny picked my shoes out too. Janice asked me if I liked the shoes Benny picked out for me. I said yes, but I didn't. I knew he was going to get what he liked anyway. After shopping, we stopped and had pizza for dinner and went home. When we got home, I got my tablet out and started drawing pictures. I was glad my mom had packed my drawing tablet, coloring books, puzzles, pencils, and colors for me.

Benny came in my room and said, "You better enjoy your time because after today, all that shit is going in the trash. You will have plenty of chores to do. In fact, give me all that shit right now and go clean up the bathroom." Before I could give it to him, he snatched all my stuff up and said to follow him. On the way to the bathroom, he threw my stuff in the trash. Janice was coming out of the bathroom. She asked Benny what he was doing.

He said, "Tammy is going to clean up the bathroom. Show her what to do."

Janice said, "I've already cleaned the bathroom."

He said, "She's going to clean it again, so show her what to do."

So Janice showed me how to clean up the bathroom, and then she said, "Go watch TV." I went in my room instead. I couldn't believe he threw my stuff in the trash. I lay across the bed and started talking to God. I said, *God, I really don't think she's my real mom. I think my mom made a mistake sending me here.* I said the Lord's Prayer, and I thought I would feel better, but I didn't. I went in the den and started watching TV with Benny Jr. and Belinda. Benny came in the den and turned the channel to a football game.

Benny Jr. and Belinda got up and left the room. I got up to leave too, but Benny told me to sit my ass down, and I can get up when he said I can get up. When the game went off, he told me to go to bed, and Janice will be enrolling me in school the next day. I asked Benny if I could close the door and put my pajama on. Benny said, "Yes. Just open the door back when you're done." After I put my pajamas on, I opened the door and looked in the den. The TV was off, and Benny was gone. I was so used to my mom hugging and kissing me at night before I went to sleep. We would always get on our knees together and say the Lord's Prayer.

Now I had no one. Janice hardly ever talked to me. I didn't think my mom thought it was going to be like this. I was going to keep praying to God and be my mom's big girl. I had my mom's trophy sitting on my dresser. I put it under my bed because I was scared Benny might throw it away. Sometime in the night, I got up to go to the bathroom. My room wasn't real dark because the streetlight shone in my room. When I rose up, Benny was standing in my room. I got back in the bed and put the cover over my face and started asking, *God, please protect me from Benny.* I had to use the bathroom so bad I had to get up. I pulled the cover back off my face, and Benny was gone. I said, *Thank you, God,* and ran to the bathroom. When I got back to bed, I was scared to go to sleep, so I told God I don't understand why he was in my room, and I asked if he could keep protecting me from Benny. I fell back to sleep. It wasn't long after that Janice was waking me up to get ready for school. Janice said she was enrolling me today. I didn't see Benny anywhere, so I was thinking he went to work. Before she took me and Belinda to school, Janice dropped Benny Jr. off at the day care. When she got back to the car, I told her Benny came in my room last night.

Janice said, "Oh, he was just checking on you." Janice made it sound like it was no big deal. I felt it was a big deal. I was scared of him, but I didn't say anything else. The school was right down the street from our house, so it didn't take long for us to get there. She gave me a key to the house on a chain so I could put it around my neck, and she said to keep it under my shirt. Janice said Belinda and I will be walking home from school every day. Janice said she will be at home when we get out of school, but just in case she wasn't, we could let ourself in. Then we got out of the car and walked inside the school.

Chapter 6

Belinda went to her classroom, and Janice and I went to the office to enroll me in school. This school is nothing like what I was used to. The walls had graffiti all over them, there was trash all over the floor, and students were standing in the hall talking. First, Janice had to fill out some papers. Janice told me to sit down. I told her my pants were too tight. When I was sitting in the car, I felt like I couldn't breathe. Janice said it was because they were new, and I needed to break them in. I told Janice I never had that problem with my mom when she bought me new clothes.

Janice told me to shut the hell up and sit my ass down, so I did. She said, "I'm your mother. Doris was your aunt. You will do what I say, and you better start calling me Mama and never call me Janice again." I didn't say a word. I just sat there. I knew I looked a mess. My pants were too tight. I had to comb my own hair. I just brushed it back into a ponytail that was the same style I had when I saw my mom before she died. My aunt Tina showed me how to brush it and put it in a ponytail. I was glad my aunt Tina showed me how to do my hair, because Janice never tried to do anything to it.

After Janice filled out all the paperwork, she gave me some money for lunch and left. The office lady gave me a paper to give to the teacher and told me my room number was 707 and told me how to get to my class. I started walking down the hallway. All of a sudden, these boys grabbed me and shoved me into the boys' bathroom. They tried to snatch my pants down. I was fighting all of them. There were four of them, but I didn't care. I just kept fighting.

A teacher walked in. Maybe he heard me screaming, so the boys ran out. The teacher asked me if I was okay.

I didn't say anything. I picked my papers and ran home. When I got there, I tried to open the front door with my key. It didn't work, so I went to the back door and tried it. It worked. I heard some noises in Janice's room, so I went to her room. When I got there, I saw Benny on top of some woman. The woman saw me and said, "Benny, look, your daughter."

Benny looked at me and told me to go to the living room. I wanted to run back to school, but I did what Benny said. He came in the living room with a towel wrapped around his waist and said, "Why are you not at school?"

I didn't know what to say. I just looked at him. Benny said, "Take your ass back to school, and you better not tell Janice what you saw. If you do, I will beat the hell out of you, and I will kill Janice." I told him I needed to tell Janice something. Benny said, "You could tell Janice after school. Now take your ass back to school and remember what I said." I didn't say anything. I just ran back to school. I left my papers at home, but I remember the classroom number was 707. When I got back to school, there were a lot of kids outside playing. No one noticed me, so I sat down on one of the swings.

I started talking to God in my mind. I said, *Why is all this happening to me? My mom told me if I pray to you and ask you to protect me, you would. I really don't feel protected right now, or maybe you're too busy, and you haven't got to me yet.* The school bell rang, and everyone went back inside the school. I told God, *I will talk back to you later. I've got to find my class.*

When I walked into the classroom, the teacher said, "You must be Tammy." I said yes. She said, "I'm Mrs. Cooks, your homeroom teacher. Did the office give you a paper to give to me?"

I said, "Yes, I lost it."

She said, "Don't worry, I will take care of it," and told me to find a seat.

Mrs. Cooks brought me a folder and said, "We are going over the school rules right now," and she showed me where they had left off. Mrs. Cooks told me to take the folder home and read it with my parents, because I had missed the first part they talked about. I said okay. I wasn't paying attention to what Mrs. Cooks was talking about. I thought about what those boys tried to do to me. It was good my pants were tight because they weren't able to pull them down. I'd never had to fight in school, but I thought I was going to be doing a lot of fighting to protect myself. Then I thought about Benny.

I decided to not tell Janice about what I saw or what those boys tried to do to me. But I was going to ask her if I can go live with my aunt Tina. The school bell rang again. Only this time, it's time to go home. I went to Belinda's class and got her first. She was in kindergarten. Once we were outside, there was a group of girls, and they asked me if I was a new student. I said yes, then they started calling me names. They said I was ugly, my hair was nappy, my clothes were ugly, I was skinny with too little clothes on, and I had rabbit teeth. I didn't say anything. I just got Belinda's hand and walked home.

No one called me names at my old school. I didn't know I was so ugly till now. My mom always called me her pretty girl. When we got home, Janice was there. She gave Belinda a hug, but she didn't hug me. Janice asked me how I liked school. I gave her the folder, and I told her I didn't like it and asked her if I can go live with Aunt Tina. Janice said, "No. Get used to it, because you're not going back to Texas." She added, "When Benny gets home, we will go and get school supplies for you and Belinda." I didn't say anything. I just went in my room. I was glad we were getting school supplies because then I could draw again, and maybe Benny won't throw my papers and pencils in the trash. But I was not looking forward to seeing Benny.

Chapter 7

A little time went by, and Benny came home. Benny came in my room and just looked at me. He didn't say anything. My heart started beating really fast. I didn't know what he was going to do or say. Then Janice walked in. She gave Benny a kiss and said dinner was ready, so we all went to the kitchen table. Benny said to me I better not be looking, talking, or playing with boys. I didn't say anything. I just kept eating. I didn't understand why he said that, but I was going to do what he said. After dinner, we went out and got school supplies.

When we got home, I took a bath and went in my room and started looking at my school supplies. I took some of them and put them under my bed so I could draw when Benny wasn't around, then I went and watched TV with Belinda until it was time to go to bed. Belinda had her own room, but sometimes she liked to sleep with me. Benny came in my room and said it was time to go to bed and told Belinda she had to sleep in her bed. Benny asked me if I said anything to Janice about what I had seen earlier that day. I said no. Benny said if I did, he was going to beat the hell out of me and to take my ass to sleep, then he left my room.

After Benny left, I asked God, *Please forgive me for not getting on my knees to pray. Benny doesn't seem to like anything I do. I never know when he's watching me. I don't think Benny or Janice prays like my mom did. I never hear your name since I've been here. God, please protect me from Benny. I'm not strong enough to fight him. I will protect myself from the kids at school. That way, you can focus on protecting me from Benny. I love you, God. Please let my mom know I love and miss her so much.* I said the Lord's Prayer and went to sleep.

I woke up sometime that night. I had a nightmare. I dreamed Benny was beating Janice, and then he pulled out a gun and pointed it at her. I woke up before he shot her. The dream seemed so real. I looked up, and Benny was standing in the doorway looking at me. I put the cover over my face. I was scared to move. After a little while, I took the cover off my face, and Benny was gone. I started again asking God to protect me from Benny. *I think he wants to hurt me. Janice never talks to me. I think she doesn't like me either.* I just lay there. I must have fallen asleep, because Janice was waking me up to get ready for school. It took some time to get used to the name-calling and the bullying. I learned to ignore the name-calling, and I would fight the bullies and anyone else who tried to hurt me. As time went by, Benny and Janice would fight and argue all the time like my mom and dad did in Texas. Only it was worse; they fought about drugs, money, and them seeing other people. If they argued during the day, I would take Benny Jr. and Belinda outside so they wouldn't have to hear them, and if it was at night, they would get in the bed with me.

The fighting and arguing they did made Benny Jr. and Belinda cry. Belinda would always shake and tell me she's scared. I would hold her and Benny Jr. to try to comfort them. I was just as scared as they were, but I couldn't show them that. One morning Belinda and I were walking to school. Belinda walked ahead of me with her friends. Then they ran the rest of the way. I could see her going into the school building. Right when I got ready to cross the street to get into the school, a car pulled up in front of me. It was a man with a clown mask on.

He said, "Come here, little girl." I didn't say anything to him. I just took off running to the school. Once I was at the door, I turned around and looked back, and he was gone. He scared me really bad, but I was glad I was safe. I went by Belinda's class to make sure she was there. And she was there, and I decided I would never let her go by herself even if she was with her friends. Then I went to my class and sat down, and I thought about what just happened. I told God, *Thank you for protecting me,* silently in my mind. The school bell rang, and I told God, *I will talk with you later.*

The school day went by fast. As soon as I got home, I told Janice about what happened. She didn't say much. She said she was glad I was safe. I thought she would call the police, but she acted like it wasn't a big deal. I went and started doing my homework. I watched TV for a little while, and then I took a bath and said the Lord's Prayer and went to sleep. I felt something on my leg; it woke me up. It was Benny feeling on my vagina. I still had my pajamas own. I screamed, and Benny put his hand over my mouth and told me to shut the hell up.

Benny said if I tell Janice he was in my room, he will kill me and Janice, and he left my room. Now I know Janice couldn't be my real mom. Why didn't she check on me at night? Why was she not concerned about anything I did? My heart was beating so fast. I didn't know what to do. I was asking God, *Please protect me from Benny. I know he wants to hurt me. I am scared to close my eyes. My mom said if I pray to you, God, you will protect me. I don't know if I'm praying the wrong way and that's why you're not protecting me, but I need your help right now.*

Now it's worse; he's touching me. I told God, *I don't know what to do. I'm scared to tell Janice. I'm scared he might really kill us. Please, God, take me out of this situation.* I stayed awake till the morning came.

Janice came in my room and said, "No school today because of the snow." My mom could look at me and could tell when something was wrong with me. I thought since Janice was my real mom, she could look at me and tell something was wrong, and I could tell her what Benny did to me last night. Then Benny walked in my room and told Janice to fix him breakfast. Benny gave me an evil look. It made my heart beat so fast. They both left my room. What Benny did made me think about something that happened to me when my mom left me with one of her friends. My mom had something to do that I couldn't be there with her. My mom's friend had three boys who were around my age. I was five or six years old at the time. After my mom left, her friend took me in her den to watch TV with her sons, and she left the room. One of the boys followed her and came back and said their mom was in her room in the bed.

Right after he said that, the boys attacked me; they knocked me down on the floor and started pulling my pants and panties down. I was screaming and fighting. All of a sudden, someone snatched one of the boys off me; it was my mom. She helped me pull my pants and panties up and asked me if I was okay. She told me to go get in the car, and she would be there in a minute. When she got in the car, she asked me again if I was okay and if they hurt me. I told her I was okay, and I asked her why they did do that to me and why didn't their mom try to help me. My mom said she talked to the boys and their mother about them trying to hurt me and told me we will never go over there again.

My mom said she was sorry that happened to me and that it will never happen again. She took me to her doctor's appointment and asked the nurses to watch me. Later that night, my mom explained to me about what to do if that ever happens again and to always tell if someone touches me on my private. My mom's not here with me right now, so I have no one to tell. I asked God if he could give my mom a message. She told me she would always be in my heart. I just won't be able to see her. *God, please tell her I need her right now to protect me from Benny. He's trying to do the same thing her friend's sons tried to do to me. Please find a way to take me from here, and I love and miss my mom so much.* I got on my knees and said the Lord's Prayer. When I opened my eyes, Benny was in my room.

Benny said, "Get your ass up off the floor, and I better not catch you praying to God again. There is no God. You have to save yourself. Now get your ass in the den and watch TV like the other kids." I went in the den and watched TV like he said. The whole time my heart was beating so fast. He left the room. I still believed in God because I believed what my mom taught me about God.

Later that night, when it was time to go to bed, I put the cover over my head and started praying to God silently so Benny couldn't hear me. I asked God to please protect me from Benny. I said the Lord's Prayer and just lay there until I fell asleep. I woke up from a nightmare. I dreamed Benny was hurting me, and no one was there to save me. I was on my left side facing the wall. I turned on my right side, and Benny was standing there by my bed playing with his penis.

He put his hand over my mouth and said, "You better not scream," and left my room.

Normally I would pray to God after Benny left my room, but I didn't feel like praying today. I just lay there till morning came, wondering why Janice wasn't coming in my room to see if I was okay. There were times I did scream before Benny could put his hand over my mouth, and she never came. It's a Saturday morning; and Benny came in my room and told me to brush my teeth, wash my face, and put some clothes on. Benny said he was going to teach me how to shovel the snow off the walkway leading to our front door. It was really hard to do, and I was freezing, but I couldn't stop till Benny said I could.

Janice came outside and said, "Tammy, go in the house."

"I will be there in a minute."

When we came in, Benny slapped Janice so hard she fell. Benny Jr. and Belinda started crying and trying to help Janice get up.

Benny told Janice, "Don't ever go against anything I've told Tammy to do." He also told her to take her ass in their bedroom. Janice took Benny Jr. and Belinda with her. Benny told me to go to the den, and he followed me. He took his belt off and started whooping me. I tried to run, but he was holding one of my hands. I screamed, and I cried real bad, and then he told me to go to my room and shut up all that damn crying. My mom never whooped me, but my dad (Uncle Ray) would, but nothing like that. I was hurting all over, including my hands from shoveling the snow. I was praying to God like my mom taught me, but it seemed like God couldn't hear me because bad things were still happening to me.

Chapter 8

Months went by. The snow was gone. When Benny wasn't there, Janice would let us go outside and play with other kids in the neighborhood. Two of my classmates lived on the same street I lived on. Janice would let me visit them, and they could visit me. I had two best friends, Tajohna and Patricia.

Tajohna and Patricia had problems at home too. They would talk about their problems sometimes, but I was too scared to talk about mine. As time went by, I started sneaking out of my window at night and going to stay with Patricia. Her mom worked at night, and she and her little sister stayed at home alone, so Benny couldn't hurt me if I wasn't there. I would always wake up before sunrise. I would run back home and climb back through my window. I thought Benny wasn't coming in my room anymore because no one said anything to me about the times when I would go and stay with Patricia at night.

One night I tried to climb out of the window, and I couldn't get it open. Benny came in my room and said, "You won't be climbing out that window anymore. I nailed it down, and you better not try any other windows." Benny continued, "I know you're sneaking out to fuck boys." Then he started whooping me with his belt. I screamed and hollered for Janice, but she never came. After he was done, he told me to take my ass to bed. After Benny left my room, I started asking God for forgiveness because I had stopped praying. I asked God, *Please come back in my life. I promise I will be a better child.*

I just lay there till I fell asleep. Morning came, and everything was the same as always. I went to school. Benny and Janice went to work. I would come home, do my chores, and do my homework.

Benny would still come in my room at night and do whatever he wanted to me. I would fight him, but he was stronger than me. One night Benny was in my room, and Janice called him. Benny jumped up and ran out of my room. I had started sleeping in my clothes because I had decided I was going to run away. I didn't know when and where I was going to go just yet. So when Benny went to see what Janice wanted, I ran out of the back door. I ran to my friend Tajohna's house and knocked on her bedroom window. Tajohna looked out of the window and told me to go the front door. When she opened the door, her mom was there too. I asked if I could stay the night. Tajohna's mom asked me what's wrong and if my mom knew I was there. I said no, and I said she won't mind. Tajohna's mom walked me back home. She rang the doorbell, and Benny came to the door.

Tajohna's mom asked Benny if everything was okay. Benny said everything was fine. "Tammy does this all the time. Thank you for bringing her home." I went in my room, and Benny followed me. Benny said, "Don't ever do that shit again," and started whooping me with his belt. After Benny whooped me, he told me to take my ass to bed. So I did. I didn't go to sleep right away. I started talking to God. I asked him, *Why are you letting this happen to me? My mom told me you're a protector, and right now, I'm not being protected. I guess you're busy helping someone else.* I decided to say the Lord's Prayer anyway and fell sleep thinking about my mom.

Chapter 9

One night Belinda and I were watching TV in the den. Benny Jr. was in Janice's room with her. I looked over at the window; the curtain was open a little bit. I could see a man looking at me. I grabbed Belinda and ran to tell Janice. Janice told us to stay in her room while she went and checked to see if anyone was there. When Janice came back, Benny was with her, and Janice said she didn't see anyone. Benny said, "It was probably one of those boys Tammy goes to school with." I believe it was Benny.

One evening after school, I was sitting on the front porch watching our neighbors next door playing football. The next thing I knew, Benny snatched me up and said, "What did I tell you about looking at boys?" and told me to take my ass in the den. Then he took his belt off and whooped me and told me to take my ass outside and sit back on the porch. While sitting on the porch, one of the boys came over and asked me if I was okay. I had my head down because I was scared to look. I guess Benny was watching because he came outside and told the boy, "Don't say anything to Tammy, and get your ass out my yard."

Benny said, "So you have been talking to boys." I didn't say anything. Benny said, "Take your ass back to the den. You don't listen." He whooped me again. After he was done, he said, "Go to your room." I couldn't come out till he said I could.

Janice came in my room and said, "If you just do what Benny says, he wouldn't whoop your ass so much." I wanted to tell her what Benny was doing to me so bad. Since she never would come in my room when Benny was there, I began to think she knew what he was doing to me, and she didn't care. So I kept my mouth shut about it.

Janice told me to go back in the den and watch TV. Later that night, Janice told us to go to bed. Belinda asked Janice if she could sleep with me. Janice said yes. I was glad because Benny wouldn't come in my room if Belinda was there. Well, this particular night, Belinda peed in the bed. I woke Belinda up and washed her off, put some clean clothes on her, then put her in her bed. I did the same for me. Instead of getting back in my bed, I got a pillow and a blanket to sleep on the couch in the den. I went back to sleep. A nightmare woke me up. When I looked up, Benny was naked and was about to get on top of me. I was able to get up before he could.

I ran out of the back door into the garage. I wanted to run to Patricia's house, but I didn't have any shoes on. The car door was unlocked, so I lay down in the back seat. I started saying the Lord's Prayer, and then I decided to go back in. I was glad I left my key around my neck because Benny had locked the door. I went back and lay on the couch, praying to God to not let Benny come back and hurt me. I guess God heard me that time because Benny didn't come back. I told God thank you. I must have fallen asleep because Janice was waking me up to get ready for school.

Janice asked me why I slept on the couch. I told her Belinda peed in the bed. She said Belinda and I needed to take a bath before we went to school. Benny had already left for work. Janice and Benny Jr. were headed out of the door. After she woke me up, Belinda and I took a bath, ate some cereal, and went to school. I was glad it was Friday. On weekends, Benny didn't come in my room because Benny and Janice would go out on Fridays and Saturdays. When Benny would work on a Saturday, Janice would let me go and hang out with friends.

I had learned the neighborhood well, and I'd been hanging out with a gang of girls. I even learned how to catch the city bus and go anywhere we wanted to go. My friends had taught me the street life. Some Saturdays we would have street fights. We fought for money. I would save my lunch money in case someone called me out. You win, you double your money. Once other kids found out you're a good fighter, the bullies would leave you alone, and all the name-calling would stop. I earned that right. Now I just needed to figure out a way to hurt Benny.

Chapter 10

One Saturday my gang and I caught the city bus to the city park. We decided to check out the neighborhood around the park. We walked up on five bikes lying in someone's yard, and there were five of us, so we decided to steal them. Each member grabbed a bike. By the time we got on the street, some Mexican boys came out of the house. They chased us for a while, but they couldn't catch us. We saw a city bus about to stop and pick up some people. We left the bikes in someone's yard and jumped on the bus. We all went home after that.

When I arrived home, Janice asked me if I was hungry. I said yes, so I went and washed my hands and face and sat down at the dinner table. Janice fixed me and her a plate. While eating, Janice told me we would be home alone that night because she and Benny were going out for the evening. I said okay. After I finished cleaning the kitchen, I went in the living room and started watching TV with Belinda and Benny Jr. Benny and Janice said good-bye and left. Whenever we were left alone, we would run through the house playing hide-and-seek.

Benny Jr. had to go to the bathroom. I went with him because I had to wipe him. All of a sudden, Belinda ran in the bathroom and slammed the bathroom door. The doorknob on the outside of the door fell off. I couldn't get the door open. Belinda and Benny Jr. started crying. I told them it will be okay. I started playing games with them where they had to guess what kind of animal I was. When we got tired of playing games, we all got in the bathtub. Benny Jr. and Belinda lay on me and fell asleep while I prayed out loud to them so they could learn how to pray like me. I said the Lord's Prayer over and over, till I fell asleep.

Sometime that night, Janice woke us up. Janice was laughing and said Benny was going to fix the doorknob so that doesn't happen again and told us to go get in our beds. I had to go through the den to get to my bedroom. Benny was standing in the den with his belt in his hand.

Benny said, "Tammy, why did you break the doorknob?" I said I didn't. It fell off when Belinda slammed the door. He grabbed my hand and started whooping me. When he was done, he said, "Don't ever lie on Belinda again, and take your ass to bed." So I did.

When I got in my bed, I started talking to God. I asked him, *What do I need to do to get you to take me out of this situation? My mom said you see everything. It doesn't seem to matter whether I'm a good girl or a bad girl. Bad things keep happening to me. I'm starting to think I'm supposed to take care of myself. I just don't know how to protect myself from Benny.* I said the Lord's Prayer and fell asleep, thinking of a way to kill Benny. I woke up early that morning before anyone got up. I had a nightmare about Benny hurting me, and no one came to save me.

It was Sunday, and we were all at the table eating breakfast. Benny told me I had to iron all his work clothes that day and to start after breakfast. I washed the dishes and went to the laundry room and started ironing Benny's work clothes. Janice came in the laundry room and said to me, "Tammy, Benny is gone. I will finish ironing Benny's clothes, and you go watch TV in the den." I said okay and left. While I was watching TV, I looked through the window, and Benny was standing there looking at me. I was not sure how long he was standing there.

He came inside and said to me, "Tammy, you done ironing my work clothes?"

I said, "No, Janice said she would finish ironing them."

Benny said, "Oh, she did!" and left the room. Then I heard them arguing about Janice taking up for me. That made me feel bad because it was my fault, and I knew he will hurt Janice. Benny Jr. got in my lap and held on to me, and Belinda laid her head on me. I just sat there holding on to them, until they stopped arguing. Benny came in the den and told Belinda and Benny Jr. to leave the room, and they did.

Benny said to me, "When I tell you to do something, you better do it. I don't give a damn. What Janice says, you do what I say, end of discussion. Go back and finish ironing my work clothes." So I did.

Chapter 11

Some time went by. Benny and Janice decided to go out and hang out with some of their friends. While we were in the den watching TV, I heard someone trying to open the back door. I thought it was Benny and Janice. We had a window on our back door, and I saw this man trying to break in. I got Belinda and Benny Jr. and ran in the kitchen to call the police. While I was on the phone with the police, the man had come to the front door, trying to break it open.

I hung the phone up and called our next-door neighbor Pam. I told her what was going on. The doorbell rang. I could hear Pam saying the man was gone. "Open the door, Tammy." I opened it. I was so happy to see Pam. I was so scared. Pam made sure all the doors and windows were locked. She said it will take a while before the police got there. They took their time when it came to our neighborhood. Pam said she would stay with us until our parents came home. We sat there on the couch in the living room watching TV.

All of a sudden, someone twisted the doorknob at the front door. Pam ran to the kitchen and got a knife. There was a chain holding the door. He stuck his hand through the crack of the door, and Pam stuck the knife in his hand. He kicked the door in. As soon as that happened, police were in the yard and telling the man to lie down on the ground. Pam seemed like she was ready to fight if he would have made it in. Benny Jr. and Belinda were screaming and hollering the whole time. I was scared too, but I was going to protect Benny Jr. and Belinda while Pam was talking to the police.

Benny and Janice walked in. They asked me what happened. There was blood all over the front door and the porch. Janice hugged us and said she was glad we were all right. That was the first time Janice hugged me, and it felt so good. After the police left, Benny Jr. and Belinda asked Benny if they could sleep with me. Benny said yes, and he was proud of me, and I handled that situation good and told us to go get in the bed. Once Belinda and Benny Jr. were asleep, I started talking to God. I said to God, *Thank you so much for protecting us tonight. Thank you for sending Pam. I really didn't know what to do. Maybe Janice is my real mom. That hug she gave me warmed my heart. I kinda felt like my mom Doris was hugging me. It was the first time Benny said something nice to me. Please, God, change Benny into a better person and keep him out of my room at night.* Then I said the Lord's Prayer and fell asleep thinking about my deceased mom, Doris. The next day, everything went back to normal. We went to school, Benny went to work, and Janice stayed home and cleaned up the blood.

When we got home from school, Janice told us to do our homework now, because when Benny got home, we were going out to eat pizza. Benny came home and took a shower, and we headed out of the door. I got on the passenger's side of the car. Benny gave me a funny look. I knew that meant I had to sit behind him, and I did. I hated that because he would stare at me through his rearview mirror, and it would make my heart beat so fast. I only ate one piece of pizza. I had lost my appetite. Janice asked me what was wrong. I told her I was full.

Janice said okay. Benny said, "You're not full. Eat that motherfucking pizza till I say you're full," so I ate till Benny said I could stop. After that, we left. While sitting in the car, I started talking to God silently. I said to God, *I thought after what we went through with that man trying to break in, Benny had changed, but he hasn't. I have heard my deceased mom talking about the demons that walk this earth are working for the devil. My mom never discusses the devil with me, only to other adults. I'm wondering, God, is Benny a demon? Is that why you can't protect me against him?*

I looked up, and we were pulling in our driveway. I told God, *I will talk back with you tonight when I go to bed.* Later that night when I was bathing, Benny walked in the bathroom and told me to turn my head while he used the bathroom. I wasn't allowed to lock the bathroom door in case he had to use the bathroom. As soon as he left, I jumped up and put my pajamas on. When everyone went to sleep, I would put on regular clothes. I started talking to God about the devil. *I don't know much about the devil, but if there is one and Benny is a demon, could you please ask the devil to tell him to leave me alone? I'm sorry if I did something wrong to you.* Then I said the Lord's Prayer and fell asleep.

The next morning, I woke up, and I realized I didn't have any nightmares, and Benny didn't come in my room, that I knew of. I told God, *Thank you for protecting me last night. I guess the devil needed me to apologize to him for some reason. I will continue to apologize if that will keep Benny out of my room.*

Chapter 12

Months went by, and Janice took us over to Benny's mother's house. Her name was Mary, but we called her Cece. Most of the time she would come and visit us; this time we were visiting her. When we walked through the door, Belinda and Benny Jr. would run to her and give her big hugs and kisses. I didn't hug her. I still didn't really know her. But she would always say, "Hi, Tammy," and smile at me; and I would say, "Hi, Cece." Everyone sat down but Janice. Janice told us we were spending the night there because she and Benny were going out that night and didn't want to leave us home alone. She told us to be good, and she will see us tomorrow. After Janice left, we started watching a show called *Animal Kingdom*, and we all were enjoying ourselves. Then this man walked through the front door. It was Cece's husband. I had met him a long time ago, and this was my second time seeing him. The first thing that came out of his mouth was "Where did you get this ugly little thing from?" He was talking about me.

Cece said, "This is Janice's daughter." Cece said to me, "This is my husband, Willie. You can call him Papa."

Willie said to me, "You're black and skinny with nappy hair. Your sister Belinda is pretty with long beautiful hair. Maybe some of that ugliness will go away as you grow up." Willie hurt my feelings bad, but I continued watching TV. I'd never compared myself to Belinda. I just looked at her as my little sister. Overall, I was happy to be there because Benny couldn't touch me, and we weren't left alone. Willie asked Cece what's for dinner. Cece said dinner was done, and she brought him a plate to the table. Cece told us to go wash our hands, and our plate will be on the table.

While I was in the bathroom, I could smell the food; it smelled really good. When I sat down at the table, I didn't recognize what was on my plate. I asked Cece, "What kind of meat is this?" Cece said it was pig feet, turnip greens, black-eyed peas, candied yams, and hot water corn bread. I ate everything; it was delicious. After dinner, I did the dishes and started back watching TV. Cece told me to come and brush her hair. Cece was a beautiful lady with long pretty hair. Cece told me to count each stroke till I got to a hundred, and then I could stop.

Once I was done, Cece gave me a pillow and blanket and told me to sleep on the couch. Cece cut the TV off and went to her room. As I lay there, I started talking to God. I said, *Thank you for the food Cece cooked. It was delicious, and I feel safe here with Cece.* I was tired, and so I said the Lord's Prayer and went to sleep.

Cece woke me up real early that morning. It was still dark outside, and everyone else was still asleep. Cece had a bucketful of water and a towel. She had hardwood floors, and she told me to get on my knees and clean her floors. I was used to mopping but not on my knees. Cece said I needed to be done before everyone woke up. While I was scrubbing her floors, I started thinking about my deceased mom. I wondered, would I be doing all this cleaning all the time if she were alive? I was sure it probably wouldn't bother me because I loved my mom so much, and she wanted nothing but the best for me.

Cece said I was moving too slow, so I stopped thinking about my mom and just tried to hurry and get it done. When I was done, Cece said there were face towels and new toothbrushes in the bathroom, and I had to wake up Belinda and Benny Jr. When we were done, Cece said, "Come and sit down at the table and eat breakfast." When I sat down at the table, there were bacon, sausage, ham, grits, rice, eggs, and biscuits. I had never seen so much food for breakfast at one time.

Cece said, "Tell me what you want, and I will fix your plate." Breakfast was delicious. I wanted to live with Cece. After we ate, I cleaned the kitchen and bathroom. Willie told me to come and help him feed the dogs.

Willie's dogs were very friendly. They all were in cages. We would put the food outside the cage, and while they ate, we would rake the poop out of the cage and put it in a trash bag. Willie said that would be my job every time I came over there. When I was done, Cece told me to sit on the front porch till Janice came because I smelled like dog poop. When Janice got there, she asked me if I was ready to go, then she said, "What is that smell?" I told Janice Willie had me cleaning out the dog cages. Janice said, "Did he pay you?"

I said no. Janice went in the house and got Belinda and Benny Jr. and gave me ten dollars. Janice said, "Willie gave that to you for cleaning the cages," and Janice said, "Don't do that shit ever again." I didn't tell her what Cece had me doing because I liked Cece, and I wanted to come back again. When we got home, Janice told me to leave my shoes outside on the porch and take a bath. I didn't see Benny's car outside, so I felt safe. When I got out of the tub, Janice called me to the living room.

Janice said to me, "Come on, Tammy, and dance with me." Belinda and Benny Jr. were already dancing with her. While dancing, I started thinking about my deceased mom. She loved to dance too. I missed her so much. I was unhappy, and I lived in fear every day. After we stopped dancing, I started feeling better about Janice. I said to myself, *Maybe Janice does love me. She just doesn't show it all the time. Maybe she's scared of Benny too.* I wanted to tell her what Benny was doing to me at night, but I was too scared. Janice turned the TV on, and we started watching *Animal Kingdom*. That was one of our favorite shows. I wished Benny didn't live with us. I felt my life would be better.

Later when Benny came in, I heard him tell Janice he will be working nights and more hours. I immediately went in my room and started talking to God. I said, *Thank you! Thank you, God, for taking Benny out of my life. He won't be home at night to hurt me anymore, and please keep him on nights.* I was about to say the Lord's Prayer when Benny came in my room.

Benny said to me, "You must want your ass whooped, because I've already told you there is no God and no praying in this house." I didn't say anything to Benny. I just looked at him. Benny looked at me for a minute and left my room.

Chapter 13

Months went by. Benny was still working nights. I was not scared to close my eyes at night. I was starting to have less nightmares. Janice was being nicer. She let us play outside more with our friends. I was so thankful to God because I knew he was responsible for making things better. One Saturday, my friends and I were playing on the school grounds. I was teaching Belinda how to ride her bike with no training wheels. Benny Jr. was playing ball with my friend Jackie's little brother. The ball rolled down by the school door. Jackie went to go get the ball. Before she could get the ball, a Mexican boy picked it up and threw it up on the school roof, where another Mexican boy caught it. Jackie told the boy on the roof to throw the ball back down.

The boy on the roof said, "Come get it." The boy standing on the ground by Jackie said we were the ones who stole their bikes.

Jackie said, "So what are you going to do?" The boy on the roof said he's on his way down. I told Belinda and Benny Jr. to run home. Belinda started riding her bike home without falling, and Benny Jr. ran home following Belinda. There were two more of my friends there with their younger brother or sister. They all ran home; it's just me and Jackie left.

I told Jackie, "Let them have the ball and let's go."

Jackie said, "No, I'm going to wait till I get the ball back."

I told Jackie, "Please let's go. You know they roll in packs." The next thing I knew, I saw a whole gang of boys coming around the corner of the school.

Jackie said, "Let's fight one on one. No one can jump in." And she chose the boy with the ball in his hands. All of a sudden, the boy came out with a knife and started slashing Jackie's face. I took off running home. As I ran, I could see the police coming, and everyone started running. I turned around and looked for Jackie. She was lying on the ground. I ran back to Jackie, and she was holding her face. Blood was everywhere. The police told me to get back and let him help her. A police officer took my statement and took me home. When I got there, Janice was already outside. She talked to the officer, and then we went inside the house.

She said, "Do not tell Benny what happened because he wouldn't like the fact that I let you go down to the school ground to play." I said okay and went to my room.

When I got in my room, I started talking to God. I asked him, *Please take care of Jackie, and I'm sorry we stole their bikes. If we didn't do that, Jackie would be fine right now.* I got on my knees and said the Lord's Prayer because Benny wasn't home, and I really needed God's help. My mom said I should always pray on my knees. Most of the time I didn't pray on my knees because Benny would whoop me if he caught me. After that day, I never heard from Jackie again.

Chapter 14

As time passed, Benny started back working days again. Benny hadn't been coming in my room at night. But the nightmare had started back almost every night. I would still pray to God to protect me from Benny and say the Lord's Prayer like always. I made sure I ironed Benny's work clothes and did all my chores inside and outside so Benny couldn't have a reason to whoop me or say anything to me. The fighting between Benny and Janice was getting a lot worse than before. People had started breaking in our house when we weren't there. They would steal our TVs and anything else they wanted. Sometimes they would even try when we were home. Benny had guns hidden all over the house, so they were ready for anyone who tried.

One morning Belinda and I were going to play in the backyard. When I opened the back door, there was a man lying on the porch in a puddle of blood. I ran and told Janice and Benny what I saw. They immediately went back there and then called the police. Janice said the man was dead and told me to get Belinda and Benny Jr. and go in my room and stay until she came and got us. So we did. Later that night while lying in bed, Benny came in my room and put his hand on my mouth and started feeling on my private. Janice called his name, and he ran in the den as if he was watching TV. Janice came in my room and asked if I was okay. Before I could speak, Benny was in my room and started kissing Janice and told her, "Let's go in our room," so they left. I told God I thought Benny was going to stop hurting me. I asked God to forgive me because I was tired of Benny hurting me, and I had no one to help me. I'd decided I was going to kill him with one of his guns whenever I got a chance to be with him by myself. The next day, I started looking for a gun, but someone had moved them.

I couldn't find a gun, so I knew they had moved them back to their room, and I was really scared to go in their room, but I was going to take a chance as soon as I was left alone. One day Benny and Janice went to the store. They said they will be right back. As soon as they drove off, I ran to their room, and the door was locked. They had never done that before. So now I had to come up with a new plan.

Time went by, and Benny and Janice decided to go out with some friends again. Janice said we will be staying with Cece Saturday night, and she will pick us up Sunday.

I was glad to go over Cece's. We would get to eat some of her good cooking. I had made some friends who lived next door to Cece, and we would jump rope all day if we could. Cece lived in a very quiet neighborhood. Most of her neighbors were senior citizens. Well, it's Saturday morning, and we were getting ready to go over Cece's, and Benny was taking us. I hated to ride in the car with Benny because I had to sit down behind him. He would constantly stare at me through his rearview mirror. All I could think about at the time was *God, please protect me from Benny.*

We finally made it to Cece's. As soon as we walked through the door, I could smell food. Cece came out and said hello to everyone and told us to wash our hands and come and eat breakfast. Benny and Janice told Cece they had something to do so they weren't staying for breakfast, and they left. After I finished the dishes, I asked Cece if I could go next door to play with my friends. Cece said no, she had a lot of things she wanted me to do for her. If I got done early, I could go outside. Cece had me to clean out all of her closets and dresser drawers. Cece helped me the whole time.

It was pretty fun, and Cece had a lot of beautiful clothes and shoes. When we finished, I looked out of the window, and my friends were outside jumping rope. I asked Cece if I could go next door. She said, "You could play with them tomorrow. Go get the brush so you can brush my hair." While brushing Cece's hair, she told me the last time I was there, I woke her up in the night screaming and fighting in my sleep. Cece asked me, "Is anything wrong?"

I said, "No, I have nightmares at night."

Cece asked me, "What kind of nightmares?"

I told her, "I keep dreaming about this monster hurting me."

Cece said, "When you're having bad dreams like that, it means you are a bad girl." I didn't say anything. I just kept brushing Cece's hair. All of a sudden, someone knocked on the door. Cece told me to go and open the door. When I opened it, a man just walked in the house.

Cece said, "Hey, Hounddog, have a seat." Cece told me to go in the back bedroom and watch TV, so I did. The next thing I knew, Cece brought the man in the bedroom I was in. Cece told Hounddog to have fun with me and knock on the door when he was finished. I begged Cece to not leave this man with me. Cece didn't say anything. She closed the door and locked it from the outside. As soon as the door closed, Hounddog attacked me. He wasn't trying to have sex with me. He wanted to bite me, and he did. I fought him as hard I could. He was so strong. He would bite me all over. Finally he stopped and knocked on the door. Cece came and unlocked the door. Hounddog gave Cece some money and left.

Cece said to me, "This is what happens when you're a bad girl. Go in the bathroom and take a shower." When I took my clothes off, I had teeth prints all over my body.

Two of the bites had cut my skin. When I got in the shower, I didn't know if I should pray or cry. Then I started wondering were Belinda and Benny Jr. were. The last time I saw them, they were on the couch asleep. Surely they heard me screaming. After I got dressed, I looked in the living room, and they were sitting on the floor watching cartoons. Cece told me to clean up the bedroom because it was a mess from me fighting Hounddog. After I cleaned up the room, I stayed in there watching TV. I was hurting all over. Cece came in the room. Tears were rolling down my face.

Cece said to me, "Stop crying. That is what your ugly ass gets. Go in the living room and watch TV." So I did. I couldn't believe what had just happened to me. I wanted to run away so bad, but I had nowhere to go. All kinds of thoughts were going through my mind. One thing's for sure, I hated Cece and Benny. I wanted to kill them both. My body was used to hurting and being bruised all the time, and no one ever said anything. I was too scared to tell anyone. I thought about figuring out a way to kill myself so I could be with my deceased mom. For some reason, I felt that would disappoint my mom.

Night finally came. Once everyone was in bed, and I was on the couch, I started talking to God. I didn't know where to start. I told him, *I'm confused. I thought if I prayed and be a good girl, you would protect me. God, you're all I got. I love you so much. Even though all these bad things keep happening to me, I still love you, but could you please help me out of this situation?* Tears started running down my face. I started saying the Lord's Prayer, and then I cried myself to sleep thinking about my deceased mom. Cece woke me up early to scrub the floors. Cece asked me if I was mad at her about yesterday.

I didn't say anything. I just kept scrubbing the floor. Cece said, "Answer me when I'm talking to you." I said no. Cece said she didn't give a damn anyway. After I was finished, I woke Belinda and Benny Jr. up and got them ready for breakfast. I didn't go to the table. I just sat on the couch and started watching TV.

Cece said, "Get your skinny ass over here and eat." I wasn't hungry, but I wasn't going to say no, because I didn't know what she would have done to me. After breakfast, we all started watching TV. All of a sudden, emergency news flashed across the TV screen. It was trash day, and there was a dog on the loose with rabies in Cece's neighborhood. They asked everyone to stay in their home until further notice.

Cece said, "I forgot it's trash day. Tammy, take the trash can in the backyard and roll it down to the end of the yard so the trashman can pick it up."

I said, "Cece, the newspeople said don't go outside right now." Cece told me to get my ass up and do what she said, so I did. Once I got in the backyard, I asked God to please protect me from that dog. I started rolling the trash can down by the street. I didn't see the dog. Once I set it down, I could see the dog coming down the street.

Cece was at the front door. She had it open and was saying, "Run, Tammy, run!" When I got there, she closed the door on me, so I ran to the back door. The dog was barking, so I knew he was close to me. Cece had the back door open and was shouting, "Run, Tammy!" This time she let me in. Cece closed the door just in time. The dog ran up on Cece's screen door and put a hole in it. The police shot the dog in Cece's front yard. Cece was laughing the whole time. I didn't see anything funny. I thanked God for protecting me.

A police officer came to the door. He said he saw me outside taking the trash to the curve and asked if I was okay. Cece told him I was fine, and the officer left. All I could think about is why Cece was so evil. About an hour later, Janice came. On the way home, I wanted to tell Janice so bad, but I knew it wouldn't matter to her. I was sure she would have thought the situation about the dog was funny too. I really wanted to tell her about Hounddog. I thought maybe she would notice the bruises on my arms so I could tell her. Janice never paid me any attention, so I guess that was why she didn't notice.

When we got home, I took a bath and went in my room. Later that evening, Benny came in my room and accused me of stealing his drugs. I didn't know what he was talking about. I told Benny I didn't do it.

He said, "Yes, you did," and took his belt off and started whooping me. After he left my room, I thought about running away. I looked in my closet to get this box where I had been saving money to run away. I felt it was time to make my move. When I opened the box, it was empty. I just sat there. I couldn't believe it. I lay across the bed with tears rolling down my face.

Chapter 15

Some time went by, and it's a Saturday morning. Benny and Janice were arguing and fighting. Belinda and Benny Jr. were in my room with me. They were crying and scared, so I took them outside so they wouldn't have to hear them arguing. While we were sitting on the porch, my friend Patricia came by and asked me if I wanted to go and have a fight to double my money.

I said, "I don't have any money, and I've got to watch Belinda and Benny Jr." Patricia said she would give me some money; just give it back if I won, and she would help me watch Benny Jr. and Belinda. I could still hear Benny and Janice arguing.

So I decided to go. I had never taken Belinda and Benny Jr. to a street fight before. I thought anything was better than listening to their parents arguing. But it wasn't. I won my fight, but I could hear Belinda and Benny Jr. crying and screaming my name. I gave Patricia her money, and we left. On the way home, I apologized to Belinda and Benny Jr. and told them I will never take them to that place again. We stopped at the store, and I bought them some chips, soda, and candy, and I think they were okay because they had a smile on their face. We headed home after that.

As we approached our house, I could see an ambulance putting Janice inside of it. We ran to the ambulance, but Benny told us to get back. He got in the ambulance with Janice and told us to go in the house and wait till they got back. When I looked at Janice, she looked like she was dead; she wasn't moving. I started praying to God to take care of her. *She needs you right now.* Belinda and Benny Jr. started crying. I told them she will be okay. We started watching

TV. Hours later, Benny and Janice walked through the door. Belinda and Benny Jr. ran to her. She told them she was okay and needed to lie down.

They didn't say anything about what happened, but Janice's face was swollen really bad. After that day, Janice started going out a lot without Benny, and Benny would go out by himself also. We were home alone a lot. Since that day, Benny hadn't come in my room at night. I still had nightmares about Benny and Hounddog biting me. I would still pray and talk to God all the time. I started back praying on my knees like my mom taught me. My birthday was coming up. I was turning twelve. I knew it won't be a celebration like my mom would do. It was always "Happy birthday, Tammy," and that was it. Sometimes not even that.

Birthdays and holidays were just another day for me. I was happy about my birthday because I knew when I turned eighteen, I can be on my own, and I'd learned that once I turned eighteen, I could buy a gun. The thought of killing Benny and Hounddog never left my mind. Well, it's Saturday, and it's my birthday. For the first time since I'd been living here, Janice asked me what I wanted for my birthday. I told her I wanted to bake a cake. She asked me what kind. I told her chocolate, so we went to the store and got the stuff. We made the cake together. It made me think about my mom.

We went in the living room and started watching TV while the cake baked. I started to get excited about my birthday. Benny came in from work and asked Janice if she was baking a cake.

Janice said, "Yes, it's Tammy's birthday today."

Benny went in the kitchen and asked me to "Come here." Benny looked in the oven, closed the oven door, and then jumped up in the air by the stove.

Janice came in the kitchen and asked Benny, "What's going on?" Janice looked in the oven at my cake, and I did too. My cake had sunk in the middle. Janice asked Benny, "Why would you do that? It's Tammy's birthday cake."

Benny said, "Because I wanted to," and left the kitchen and went to his bedroom. Janice told me she will go and buy me a cake and then went to her bedroom. Benny and Janice started arguing about the cake. I went in the backyard and sat in one of our swings and started talking to God. I said to God, *I thought things were starting to get better. I hate I asked for a cake, and I don't like birthdays anymore. Can you please protect Janice from Benny? I'm scared he might hurt her again, and it's all my fault if something happens to her.* Then I said the Lord's Prayer.

Belinda and Benny Jr. came outside, and we started playing together. I didn't worry about the cake anymore, and Janice never said anything else about the cake. The day went on like any other day. One evening after school, I was sitting on the front porch alone. I saw our neighbor across the street. He was walking to his house. His name was Billy. I would always see him at the neighborhood street fights. Billy would always speak to me. He called me Sunshine. On the way to his house, Billy stopped for a second and said, "Hey, Sunshine," and I said, "Hey, Billy." Billy was in high school.

As Billy approached his yard, his daddy came up to him and started fussing at him about staying out all night. Billy was arguing back at his dad. Billy stopped arguing with his dad and started walking toward their front door. All of a sudden, Billy's dad called his name. Billy turned around, and Billy's dad pulled out a gun and shot Billy. He kept shooting until he ran out of bullets, and then he took off running down the streets. Billy's mom came outside and saw Billy. She started screaming. She was telling Billy, "Hold on, baby, help is coming." The rest of the family were all screaming and crying. I didn't know what to do. I knew if I went over there, I would get a whooping from Benny. So I started praying to God to take care of Billy. I said, *Please, God, don't let him die.*

It's normal to hear gunshots in our neighborhood. That was the first time I saw someone get shot. When the police and ambulance made it there, it was too late. Billy had died; they covered him up with a sheet. A police officer approached me and asked me if I saw what happened. I said yes. He said, "Where are your parents?"

I said, "They're in the house."

He said, "Go get them," and I did.

Benny and Janice followed me outside. The officer asked them for permission to talk to me. Janice said yes. I told the officer what I had seen. While I was talking to the officer, Billy's daddy was walking back to his house. I told the officer, "That's Billy's dad right there, and he shot Billy." The officer ran across the street and arrested Billy's dad. After that, the officer came back and got our phone number and said he will call us later for more information. When we got in the house, Benny asked me how I knew Billy. I said he's one of my classmates' brother.

Benny said, "You're lying." Benny said, "Go to the den," so I did. Benny said, "I'm going to ask you one more time, and it better be the truth."

I told Benny, "I am telling the truth."

Benny started saying, "I know you been going across the street at night to have sex with those boys." I told Benny I wasn't doing that. Benny took his belt off and started whooping me. Normally Benny would have to hold my hand while he whooped me to keep me from running away. This time I just stood there and took the licks. Tears did roll down my face. I didn't scream, and I didn't cry out loud. I just stood there and took it.

Benny kept hitting me with the belt. He started hitting me harder to make me cry. I just took it, and the tears stopped rolling. Finally he stopped. He said I was grounded, and I couldn't go outside. Benny told me to go to my room and not come out till he said I could. I went to my room and sat on the floor. My legs, back, and booty hurt so bad I felt like I was on fire. I looked under my bed to get the trophy my mom gave me. It was gone. I knew I wasn't supposed to come out of my room, but I did anyway. I asked Benny if he got my trophy.

Benny said, "I told you not to come out that room, and yes, I threw that motherfucking trophy in the trash, and what you gon' do about it?" I didn't say anything. I went back to my room. It felt like someone stabbed me in the heart. I sat back down on the floor. I wasn't crying, and I wasn't praying to God. I just sat there. I wanted to talk to God about what happened to Billy, but I was so mad. Janice came in the room. She said she was sorry about my trophy and asked if I wanted something to eat. I told her no.

She said, "Go in the den and watch TV. I won't let Benny whoop you for leaving the room."

I didn't say anything to Janice. I just continued sitting on the floor. Later that night when everyone went to sleep, I went and got a knife out of the kitchen and went to Benny and Janice's room. I stood in the door. I was going to stab Benny in his heart. I wanted to kill him. For some reason, my legs wouldn't move so I could go in the room. It was like someone was holding me back, so I turned around to go back to my room, and my legs moved fine. I put the knife under my mattress so if Benny came in my room, I was going to stab him.

When I got back in my room, I didn't talk to God like always, but I did say the Lord's Prayer and fell asleep thinking about my mom. How I missed her so much. I had to feel her in my heart now. I didn't have my trophy anymore.

Chapter 16

One Friday after coming home from school, there was a girl sitting in our living room. Janice was in there also. Janice said to me, "This is your big sister, Rhonda." And Janice told her, "This is your sister, Tammy." We both said hi to each other. Janice told me to take her to my room. She's going to live with us, and we had to share the room.

When we got in my room, I asked Rhonda, "How old are you?" and she said thirteen. I told her I was twelve. I asked Rhonda where she had been living since she's not living here with Janice. Rhonda said she'd been living with her grandmother, her daddy's mom, in Jefferson, Texas. She said Mama wanted her to come and see if she would like to live here.

I said, "You call Janice Mama?"

Rhonda said, "Yes, what do you call her?"

I said, "I don't call her anything. I just talk without saying her name."

Rhonda said, "Why?" I told her she's not my mom. My mom died, and before she died, my mom gave me to her. Overall, I was happy to have another sister, plus she's close to my age. After we put her stuff up, I asked her if she wanted to go outside in the backyard and play jump rope or throw the ball to each other.

Rhonda said, "No, that's for kids." I didn't say anything else to her. I started playing ball with Belinda. Belinda asked Rhonda if she wanted to play with her jacks.

Rhonda said, "That's for babies." I told Belinda I would play with her. Benny came home from work, and before he went in the house, he stopped and said hi to Rhonda. Rhonda said hi back. Then

Benny went in the house, and Rhonda did too. Belinda and I stayed outside till it was time for dinner. Later that night, after we all took our bath, Janice said it was time to go to bed, and she was going to enroll Rhonda in school in the morning. Janice said good night and went to her room. Rhonda told me she didn't want to sleep in the bed with me. I told her she can have my bed, and I will sleep on the couch. Rhonda said okay and went to bed. I got a pillow and blanket and got on the couch.

Sometime during the night, I was woken up by a nightmare. When I opened my eyes, Benny was standing in the doorway looking at me. I realized my knife was under my mattress. I was scared to move. I decided if he came near me, I was going to fight him and try to run in there with Rhonda and get my knife. Benny left the den. I got up and got on my knees and started praying to God. I told God, *I'm sorry I haven't been praying like I should. I have been so confused about a lot of things going on in my life. Please forgive me. I will do better. Thank you, God, for my sister Rhonda. Maybe Benny will leave me alone now, and, God, please don't let Benny hurt Rhonda like he hurts me.* I said the Lord's Prayer and went back to sleep.

The next morning, Belinda and I rode to school with Janice, because she had to enroll Rhonda. Janice told me to wait on Rhonda after school so we could walk home together.

Rhonda said, "Don't wait for me. The school is only half a block from the house. I can walk by myself." After school, I waited for her anyway. When she came out of the school, she said, "I thought I told you I didn't want you to wait. My friend Roger is going to walk me home."

I said okay, and Belinda and I headed home. I said to Belinda, "Rhonda knows how to make friends quick." When we got home, Janice hadn't made it in yet.

Rhonda walked through the door, and she said to me, "Don't ever wait on me again. I don't want people to know you're my ugly-ass skinny sister." I said okay. It hurt my feelings, but I was used to people calling me ugly. I started doing my homework like always and my chores. Benny had a calendar on the refrigerator; it let me know what chores I had to do every day. Today I had to rake leaves in the backyard. I asked Rhonda to help me. Rhonda said she didn't do chores. I said okay and started raking leaves. When Benny and Janice came home, Benny came outside and asked me if I told Rhonda we did chores around here. I told Benny yes, and he went back inside the house. I thought he was going to tell Rhonda to help me, but she never came out to help. I thought having a sister around, we could have a lot of fun together, but no, she didn't like me. She called me stupid all the time.

A couple of days went by, and Belinda and I were walking home from school, and I saw a bunch of people standing around watching a fight. As I got closer, I realized it was Rhonda fighting another girl. The girl was whooping Rhonda pretty bad, so I jumped in it. People started pulling us apart. Someone said, "Tammy, you know we fight one on one. Why did you jump in it?"

I told them, "Rhonda is my sister."

The girl Rhonda was fighting said, "Rhonda started it. She was calling me names, and she said she was going to beat my ass, and then she hit me." I told the girl I was sorry for Rhonda starting the fight.

Everyone broke up and headed home. As we walked home, Rhonda said she didn't need me to help her fight and told me not to do it again.

I told Rhonda, "You weren't winning, and stop making trouble."

Rhonda told me to shut the fuck up and not talk to her, so I stopped talking to her. The first couple of weeks in school with Rhonda was hard because she was always talking smack and always starting a fight. One weekend, Benny and Janice went shopping. They took Benny Jr. with them. Rhonda, Belinda, and I were watching TV. The doorbell rang, and Rhonda answered it. It was Rhonda's friend Roger.

Rhonda said, "Come in, Roger." She told us to go to the den and watch TV.

Belinda told Rhonda, "My daddy does not allow boys over here." Rhonda told her to shut up and go in the den.

I told Rhonda, "Belinda is right. Benny does not want boys here." Rhonda told me to shut up and go in the den also. Belinda and I kept peeking around the corner. They lay down on the couch and started kissing.

Belinda said, "Whooo! I'm going to tell my daddy." Rhonda kept telling us to go in the den. Roger said he was leaving because Belinda and I won't give them any privacy, so Roger left.

After Roger left, Rhonda said she hated us, and she's going to tell her grandmother to come and get her. Well, when Benny and Janice came in, they bought pizza. We all sat down at the table and started eating. I was hoping Belinda didn't say anything, but she did.

Belinda said, "Rhonda had a boy over here, and they were kissing in the living room."

Benny said, "Is this true, Rhonda?"

Rhonda said, "Yes, I have boys over my house in Texas, and my grandmother doesn't mind."

Benny said, "I mind, and if it happens again, I will beat your ass."

Rhonda told Benny, "If you touch me, my daddy will beat your ass."

Benny told Janice to pack Rhonda's shit and go take her to the bus station. She might be running things in Texas, but she's not running a damn thing here. Rhonda said good; she didn't like it here anyway. Then Benny asked me why I didn't say anything.

Belinda said, "Daddy, Tammy and I did tell her."

Benny said, "I'm talking about telling me." I didn't say anything. Benny said, "You don't have nothing to say?" I still didn't respond. Benny told me to take my ass to the den. "You know what time it is."

Janice said, "Don't whoop her. It's not her fault." Benny told Janice to shut the fuck up.

I went to the den, and Benny followed me. Benny asked me where my boyfriend was. "I know you have one too. You're just sneaky with yours." I told Benny I didn't. He took his belt off and started whooping me. He said he was going to whoop me until I started screaming. I started praying to God silently to help me. I didn't move. I just took the licks. Belinda came and got behind me so Benny couldn't hit me. Benny told Belinda to move. Belinda wouldn't move; she grabbed me around my waist and begged her daddy to stop. Belinda was crying so bad.

Benny stopped and left the room. I turned around and hugged Belinda, and I started crying with her. I told Belinda thank you, and we sat down on the couch. Rhonda came in the room and said it was Belinda's fault. She should have kept her mouth shut. I told Rhonda to leave her alone. I wanted to fight Rhonda, but I knew it would be a waste of time, and I didn't want to hurt my sister regardless of how she treated me. We started watching TV. We could hear Benny and Janice arguing about Rhonda. Benny wanted Rhonda out of the house right now.

While Benny and Janice were arguing, Rhonda went and got the phone book and then called the bus station to find out when the next bus headed to Texas was leaving. Rhonda carried herself like a grown person. I think that was why she never wanted to play with Belinda and me. Even though Rhonda was mean to me, I wanted to go back to Texas with her so I could get away from Benny. I didn't ask Janice because I was scared Benny would whoop me for asking, and I didn't have any money to ride the bus. Rhonda called her grandmother and asked her to buy her a ticket at the bus station because she wanted to come home. Rhonda's grandmother told her when she gets to the bus station, the ticket will be paid for. Then Rhonda went to Benny and Janice's room and told Janice she needed her to take her to the bus station in the morning.

Benny said, "I'm not buying you a ticket home."

Rhonda said, "It's already paid for."

Benny said, "Your smart-ass mouth is going to make me whoop your ass." Rhonda left the room and called the police on Benny. Before she could say something, Benny grabbed the phone from her and told the police it was an accident.

Benny told Rhonda he was glad she was leaving. Rhonda went in my room and started packing her clothes. Janice came in my room and told Rhonda she will take her to the bus station in the morning. Rhonda told Janice she needed to leave Benny and asked, "Why you let him beat on Tammy all the time?"

Janice told Rhonda, "It's Tammy's fault why Benny whoops her ass," and left the room. I didn't say anything. I just kept watching TV.

Later that night while lying on the couch, I started wondering why Janice saved Rhonda from Benny, and she had never saved me.

I started talking to God about the situation. I said, *God, I get a whooping for everyone else's mistake. I'm not allowed to make Cs at school, only As and Bs. Benny doesn't understand it's hard to concentrate in school when he's coming in my room at night to hurt me. No one knows I have to live with pain every day on the inside and the outside of my body. I know you know, God, you see everything, and I guess you have no control of Benny. God, you're all I have, and that is why I talk to you so much.* I started crying, so I said the Lord's Prayer and closed my eyes because I never knew when Benny was watching me.

Chapter 17

The next morning, Janice took Rhonda to the bus station. I went with them. Benny took Belinda and Benny Jr. over Cece's. When we got home, Benny wasn't there. Janice told me she was going out to hang with her friend Melissa. About an hour later, the doorbell rang. Janice told me to go and let Melissa in the house, so I did. Melissa told Janice, "Come on, let's go." Janice asked me if I was going to be okay. I told her yes, and they left. Some hours went by, and Benny came home.

Benny asked me, "Where is Janice?" I told him she left with Melissa. Benny said okay and went in his room. Benny came back in the den and asked me who Janice left with again. I told Benny Melissa again. Benny said I was lying; he just got off the phone with Melissa. I told Benny Melissa came in the house, and I talked to her.

Benny said, "I'm going to ask you one more time. Who did Janice leave with?" I said Melissa. Benny took his belt off and started hitting me with it. I stood there and took the licks. Benny said, "I'm going to whoop you till you tell me the truth." The licks got harder and harder. I couldn't take it anymore.

I screamed out to God. I said, "God, please help me!" Tears started pouring down my face. I kept calling, "God, please help me! I'm telling the truth!" Then Benny stopped and left the room. I started saying the Lord's Prayer, and I thanked God for making Benny stop. I went and lay across my bed. My body felt like it was on fire. I asked God to please bring Janice home. I couldn't understand why Melissa would lie to Benny. School was out for the summer, so Benny left Belinda and Benny Jr. at Cece's that night. Benny came in my room and said, "Make yourself a sandwich for dinner," and said he would be back home later and left. I went in the den and started watching TV. I fell asleep. Benny woke me up and asked me if Janice had been home or if she had called. I told him no, and he went to his bedroom. Benny told me to go get in the bed. When I got in my room, I got on my knees and started praying. I asked God, *Please take care of Janice and bring her home. Please do not let Benny come in my room.* I said the Lord's Prayer and fell asleep thinking about Janice. That morning when I woke up, I thanked God because Benny didn't come in my room last night to hurt me.

Then I went to see if Janice had come home. Janice wasn't there, so I went to see if her car was still in the garage, and it was. I was sure Benny had left for work. I took a bath and ate a bowl of cereal and started watching TV. I was worried about Janice; she had never stayed out all night unless she's with Benny. The day went by. Benny came in from work, and he asked me if I had heard from Janice. I told Benny no. Benny went and took a shower. After that, he asked me what I wanted to eat. I told Benny it didn't matter; whatever he wanted.

This was the first time Benny had been nice to me. I thought he's worried about Janice too. I prayed my dream didn't come true about Benny killing Janice. About an hour later, Benny came in with some food from McDonald's. Now I knew something was wrong. We never got McDonald's from him. If we got it, Janice had to buy it. Benny did not like fast food unless it's pizza. A couple of days went by; still no Janice. I was still praying and asking God to bring her home. One evening when Benny came home from work, Cece, Belinda, and Benny Jr. were with him. Benny Jr. ran through the house looking for Janice.

Benny Jr. asked me where his mama was. I told Benny Jr. I didn't know. Belinda didn't say much. She sat on the couch beside me. Cece had some bags in her hands and took them to Belinda's room. Benny said Cece was going to stay with us until Janice came home. I hated that, and I hated Cece. Cece came in the den and sat down with us. Benny told Cece he will be back later. Cece told me Janice left because she was probably sick of me. Benny and Janice had a good life until I moved in. I didn't say anything. I just went to my room. Belinda and Benny Jr. followed me.

Weeks went by, and we still hadn't heard from Janice. One day I heard Cece tell Benny she was ready to move back to her house. Cece said she would take Belinda and Benny Jr. but not me. I was glad to hear that. Benny said he was going to put me in foster care. I didn't know what foster care was, but I was ready to go. Benny had stopped coming home too; only when Cece said we needed something. Cece drank a lot of beer, so she would fall asleep early and sleep all night after Belinda and Benny Jr. went to sleep. I would leave and go see if I could find Janice.

I knew her hangout spots because there were times she would take me with her. I wasn't scared to be on the streets at night. There were always kids roaming the streets. I guess they had problems like me. Besides that, I was so ugly I didn't think anyone noticed me. I had no luck in finding her, so I stopped roaming the streets and stayed home at night praying to God to bring her home. Cece told Benny this was going to be her last week there, and he needed to make arrangements for me to live somewhere. Benny told Cece he had an appointment next week with the foster care people.

I prayed to God as always, and I asked him to watch over me because I was going to run away. I was going to try to make it to Texas, before foster care came and got me. I said the Lord's Prayer and went to sleep. I was woken up that morning by Janice; she was hugging and kissing me. I hugged and kissed her back. I was so happy to see her. Belinda and Benny Jr. were with her. Benny came in the room and told us to get dressed so we can take Cece home. Benny seemed to be just as happy as we were. Benny was so happy to see Janice, he didn't notice I wasn't sitting behind him in the car.

I prayed to God silently in my head, *Thank you, God, for bringing Janice home, and please keep my family happy like it is right now. I will call Janice Mama to make her happy, and please continue protecting me from Benny. Amen.* Benny took Cece home and then took us to the zoo. After that day, I didn't hear Benny and Janice arguing very much, and Benny had stopped coming in my room. The nightmares hadn't stopped, but not as much. One Saturday morning, Benny and Janice said they had a surprise for us after we ate breakfast. We got dressed and got in the car.

Chapter 18

Benny still hadn't said anything about sitting behind him in the car, so I would always sit behind Janice. I finally could relax when riding in the car. I thanked God for that too. Benny pulled into the driveway of this two-story brick home.

Janice said, "This is our new home." I was like wow! It was way better than the house we lived in. We got out of the car and went into the house. When you first walked in, there was a staircase. You could either go upstairs or downstairs to the basement.

Janice said, "Belinda and Tammy, your bedrooms are in the basement." Belinda and I ran down to the basement and picked our rooms. Benny Jr.'s room was upstairs across from his parents The house was beautiful all over and a lot bigger than our old home. Janice said we were going to start moving that day, and we were going to stay with Cece while they moved everything in. I asked Janice if I could stay and help them move. She said yes. If she would have said no, I was going to run away. Belinda and Benny Jr. didn't want to go to Cece either. So we all went home and started packing. We spent the whole day packing.

Janice told us we were going to stay in our old house tonight, and tomorrow they will rent a truck and move everything. Janice told me our new home was in Colorado Springs. I was familiar with Colorado Springs because sometimes our family would come and visit. Benny and Janice would take them to Colorado Springs to see the mountains and do other activities they had there. Later that night while lying in bed, I started thinking about our new house and the neighborhood. There were only five houses built, but they were in the process of building more.

There were no stores close, and city buses did not run out there. Then I started talking to God. I said, *Thank you for our new home. It's really nice. Now I'm even farther away from everyone. My room is down in the basement, and if Benny starts coming in my room again, I have nowhere to run. I don't know if Janice ever heard me scream at night. She surely won't hear me now. My room doesn't have windows, so I can't escape that way, and the house has an alarm system, so they would know if I left. Overall, God, please continue protecting me from Benny.* I said the Lord's Prayer and went to sleep.

The next day came. Benny and Janice's friends came to help us load up the truck. While we were moving the furniture in our new house, a group of white people pulled up in trucks with guns and said, "You niggers don't belong in our neighborhood," and started shooting their guns in the air. Benny and his friends started arguing with them, and they went to their cars and got their guns. The white people drove off and said they would be back. They didn't come back that day, but they did come back another day while we weren't there.

We came home one day, and someone busted our windows out of our home. They spray-painted on the walls inside and out. It read, "No niggers allowed in our neighborhood." They cut up our furniture and our mattresses and broke or ripped up everything else. I started thinking maybe my old neighborhood wasn't so bad; we never had anything like that happen to us. Benny and Janice called the police. They just took pictures and did a report and left. Benny told Janice he knew it's the people in the neighborhood who did it.

Benny said, "I will get my revenge."

I didn't know what happened, but it wasn't long after that all those white families moved out and black families moved in. I was glad, because I was scared they were going to kill us. Summer was over, and school was about to start. It's a Sunday night, and I was in my room talking to God. I was able to pray on my knees a lot more now because my room was farther away from Benny and Janice's room. I was telling God, *Even though we are living better, I'm still scared of Benny, and I still want to kill him. I don't know how to find*

Hounddog, but I still want to kill him too. So I have decided I will kill Cece for letting Hounddog hurt me. If I'm still living on my eighteenth birthday, I will buy a gun and do it then. God, I don't know how you feel about what I'm going to do to Benny and Cece, but that's what I'm going to do. I pray when Janice enrolls us in school tomorrow, the school is better than my old one. If not, I'm ready this time for whatever comes my way. Plus I'm going to carry a knife in my sock for protection. I said the Lord's Prayer and went to sleep.

Chapter 19

Morning came, and we were headed to school to be enrolled. Belinda went to a different school, but it was only across the street from mine. We still had to walk home from school. It was about seven blocks from our home. We enrolled Belinda first. Her school was so nice, clean, and quiet. When we arrived at my school, it was the same way. I didn't see any black kids at Belinda's school or mine. Maybe when we started school tomorrow, we will see some then. Benny Jr. went to his old school; it was close to Janice's job. After Janice enrolled us, we went school shopping.

This time Benny didn't go with us, so we all had fun with Janice; she even let me pick out my own clothes. When we got home, while I was putting up my clothes, Benny came in my room and wanted to see my clothes. He made me try them on for him. We had our own bathroom in the basement, so I went to the bathroom to change. My heart was beating so fast. While I was in the bathroom, I heard Janice's voice. The laundry room and den were in the basement also. Janice asked Benny what he was doing. He told Janice he was waiting on me to put on my new clothes to see how they fit. Janice told me I didn't have to show Benny anything and I could go back in my room and put my clothes up, so I did. Benny and Janice went back upstairs. I could hear them arguing. I was so happy Janice took up for me. I was also scared, because the old Benny was starting to come back. I could tell by the way he looked at me. Later while we were at the dinner table, Benny told me I will have a lot more chores to do now.

Benny said, "I will post your list of chores on the refrigerator, and you will start tomorrow after school." I said okay. Sometime in the night, I was woken up by a nightmare. I got up and cut the light on to go to the bathroom, and Benny was coming down the stairs. I ran in the bathroom and locked the door. I started asking God, *Please protect me from Benny.* If I had to stay in the bathroom till morning, I was going to do that to keep Benny away from me. Then I heard Janice. She said, "Benny, what the fuck are you doing down here?"

Benny said he thought he heard something, and he was looking around. Janice knocked on the bathroom door and asked me if I was okay. I came out of the bathroom and told her I was fine.

Benny said, "She's fine. Quit babying her."

Janice said, "You better not be down here trying to mess with her." Benny hit Janice so hard she fell on the floor. Benny said to Janice, "Get your ass up and go to the bedroom," and told me to take my ass to bed. They went back upstairs, and I went to my room. I could hear them fighting upstairs.

I got down on my knees and started praying to God to protect Janice. *I'm scared he's going to kill her. I think Cece is right. I bought this problem to Janice by coming here. Please, God, take me away from this situation before Benny kills Janice and me.* The noise woke up Benny Jr. He came and got in the bed with me with tears running down his face. I asked God, *Please make them stop fighting.* After a while, they did. Benny Jr. fell asleep. I said the Lord's Prayer and stayed awake till morning. That morning Janice came downstairs, her face was swollen.

She asked me if Belinda and I would be okay if we walked to school today. I hugged her and told her, "I'm sorry for getting you in trouble."

Janice said, "You didn't do anything wrong," and gave me some money for lunch for Belinda and me. As Belinda and I walked to school, all I could think about was *I pray Janice will be okay, and I don't think I'm going to be able to wait till I'm eighteen to kill Benny. I need to figure out a way now or run away so he will quit hitting Janice.* When we got to Belinda's school, I walked her to her class so I would know where she's at. Then I went to my school. I still didn't see any black kids, and everyone was friendly. No one was calling me names, and no one tried to fight me. I tried real hard to focus in class, but all I could think about was what happened last night. Looking at Janice's face let me know Benny hurt her pretty bad. I didn't understand why Janice won't leave him. Maybe she's like me; she had nowhere to go. If this was what it's like being married, I never wanted to be married. My dad (Uncle Ray) treated my mom the same way.

The school day went by fast. Belinda was outside her school waiting for me. On our way home, she asked me why her dad was always fussing at and hurting her mom. Belinda said Cece told her it was because of me. Belinda told me she loved me, but she wanted me to move back to where I came from so Benny would stop hurting her mom. I told Belinda I was sorry, and I will find a way to get back to Texas. Belinda made me feel really bad, but I didn't show it. I told Belinda things will get better and I loved her.

When we got home, Benny was there. They both acted like nothing had happened. Benny bought Benny Jr. a toy truck and Belinda a Barbie doll. I didn't get anything, but I was used to that. I did my chores like always. I didn't have homework, so I spent the rest of the evening in my room drawing and talking to God.

As time went by, Belinda and I didn't get along anymore. She started fighting me like her daddy fought Janice. She even pulled a knife on me. I would fight her back to protect myself or to make her stop, but never hard enough to hurt her.

We had a big deck in our backyard. I spent a lot of time there. It was very peaceful. No cars passing by and no police sirens, like our old neighborhood. I would talk to God. I would say, *I'm the problem here. I'm making everyone miserable by just being here. I really don't know what to do. Can you help me come up with a plan to get away? I'm out here in the middle of nowhere. I don't want to kill myself, but it looks like that is my only way out.* I said the Lord's Prayer and went in the den and started watching TV.

Chapter 20

Months went by, and one Saturday morning, Janice woke me up. She said, "Get up, Tammy, and put some clothes in a trash bag for you, Belinda, and Benny Jr. I'm leaving Benny today. We've got to go to the bus station before we miss the bus. We are going to California to live with Ray." I jumped up and started throwing our clothes in the trash bags. I was so happy. We were finally getting away from Benny. Belinda wasn't happy. She didn't want to leave her daddy, but Janice didn't give her a choice. The whole time I was packing, I was thanking God.

When we got to the bus station, Janice bought our tickets and told us to run to the bus because it was about to leave. Benny Jr.'s bag busted as he was running. I stopped to help him pick up the clothes. Benny Jr. looked down and saw the clothes were a bunch of panties and said, "I'm not picking that up. That's nasty." And he ran to the bus. I fell out laughing. Janice said, "Run, Tammy, here comes Benny." I took off running to the bus. As soon as I got on the bus, the bus driver pulled off. I saw Benny running behind the bus, but we kept going.

I was so happy. I was thinking at last we were safe. All of a sudden, the bus driver stopped. Benny had blocked the bus with his car at the stop sign. Benny made the bus driver open the door for him. The bus driver was fussing at Benny. Benny ignored him and started begging Janice to get off the bus. I started praying to God, *Please don't let Janice change her mind.* The bus driver said if Benny didn't get off the bus, he was going to call the police. Janice told Benny she wasn't getting off the bus. So Benny got off the bus and moved his car.

I said, *Thank you, God, for answering my prayers. California, here we come.* I couldn't wait to see my daddy, I mean Uncle Ray. On the way to California, I felt Janice and I got closer. She talked to me. She even told me stories about my deceased mom, and she made me laugh. I was so grateful. After about two days, we pulled into the bus station. I saw Uncle Ray waiting for us. When we got off the bus, the first person I saw was Benny. My heart dropped. Janice hugged and kissed Benny like nothing ever happened. I was shocked. Benny told Janice he had been there since yesterday.

I hugged my uncle Ray, but I wasn't happy to see him anymore. We all got into Uncle Ray's van. Benny was telling Janice how much fun he had with Uncle Ray. I thought about the situation. My uncle Ray was just like Benny. He hurt my mom the same way when she was living. When we got to Uncle Ray's house, Uncle Ray asked me about my sad face. I didn't say anything. In fact, I didn't talk to God the whole time we were there. We stayed for two days. When we got in the car to leave, Benny made me sit behind him. I didn't talk or pray on the way home, like always.

When Benny stopped to get gas, Janice went and paid for it. Benny said to me, "You thought you won Janice over, but you didn't, and I got something for you." I didn't know what Benny was talking about, but I knew it wasn't good. In my mind, Benny can't hurt me no worse than he already had. The best thing he could do for me was to kill me. That would solve my problem, and everyone could go back to being happy. While sitting in the back seat of the car, I started talking to God silently to myself. I said, *God, I'm sorry I haven't been praying. I was so disappointed to see Benny when I came off the bus. I thought my life was about to change for the better. Janice did all that running from Benny for nothing. I asked God, Please protect me from Benny. I don't know what he has planned for me, and please forgive me for not praying or talking to you. I love you, God.* I said the Lord's Prayer and laid my head on the door and fell asleep. I was woken up by Janice.

Janice was asking me, "What's wrong?" I told her I didn't know what she was talking about. Janice said, "While you were asleep, you were fighting someone in your sleep. We had to pull the car over so we could calm you down." Janice said, "Tammy, tell me about your dream." Benny told Janice to get her ass back in the car. She asked me again what I was dreaming about. I could see Benny giving me an evil look in the rearview mirror. I told Janice I was dreaming about a monster trying to hurt me. Janice said okay and left the conversation alone.

Chapter 21

When we made it home, it was still dark. Benny told Belinda and Benny Jr. to go and get in their beds. Benny told me to start ironing his work clothes. While I was up ironing, everyone else was sleep. I was used to ironing, so it didn't bother me. That was better than Benny hurting me. Later that morning, Janice asked me if I had been ironing the whole time they were asleep. I said, "Yes. I'm almost finished." Janice said I could go lie down when I finished.

Before I could lie down, Benny came in my room and said, "After you're done washing the breakfast dishes, you need to go in the backyard and scrub our patio down." Janice tried to help me with the dishes, but Benny told her to leave me alone. I can do them by myself. Benny told Janice to go get dressed. He was taking them to the lake. Janice asked Benny why I couldn't go. Benny said he had things he wanted done before he goes to work tomorrow and before we go to school. Benny told Janice I got behind on my chores when we went to California. Janice didn't say anything. Before they left, Belinda came and told me she was glad I wasn't going and I didn't belong here anymore. Benny Jr. would always come give me kisses and hugs no matter what the situation was. It didn't bother me. I liked being by myself. Once everyone left, I went in my room and got on my knees and said the Lord's Prayer. I got the list of chores off the refrigerator and did all of them, then I took a shower and fell asleep watching TV. I must have slept really hard because when I woke up, everyone was home and asleep in their beds. I got in my bed and went to sleep too.

The next day was Monday. Janice took us to school so she could explain why we weren't there. After that, everything went back to normal. One day Janice took Belinda and Benny Jr. over Cece's. I stayed at home. Benny came home from work. I was downstairs in the den. Benny came downstairs and told me to go to my room. Benny came in my room and said, "I picked this house out just for you. Nobody can hear you down here, and you have nowhere to run." Then he pulled his pants down. I tried to run out of the room. Benny threw me on the bed and tried to take my pants off. I started screaming. Benny put his hands over my mouth and told me to shut the fuck up. Benny pulled his private out and tried to pull my pants down again. I heard the front door open. Instead of Janice coming downstairs, she went upstairs. That gave Benny enough time to pull his pants back up and go upstairs where Janice was. I didn't know what he told Janice, but she came downstairs and asked me if I was hungry. She was getting ready to cook. Janice told me she and Benny were going to a party and asked if I would be okay. I said yes.

After they left, I started talking to God as always. I said, *God, I don't understand why Janice can't see the fear on my face when Benny is around or why she would go back to someone that hurts her physically all the time. God, I wonder if I tell her what Benny has done to me, will she believe me, or if I tell her, will Benny really kill us? I guess I will keep my secret to myself. God, could you please tell my mom I love and miss her so much? God, thank you for saving me from Benny today. I know it was you that made Janice come through that door.*

I started watching TV until I fell asleep. As time went by, I became numb to everything that would happen to me. My thirteenth birthday came and left. No one said happy birthday. I really didn't think they knew it was my birthday. I figured fifteen or sixteen, I'll be ready to run away, if I'm still alive. Spring break finally rolled around, and my sister Rhonda came to visit us again. This time Rhonda had given birth to a baby girl. I was so shocked, but Rhonda had always carried herself like an adult. I was sure she's a good mommy. Even though Rhonda was always mean to me, her presence meant a lot.

Benny won't be coming in my room at night. I gave Rhonda my room. I stayed in Belinda's room with her. By the third day,

Benny wanted Rhonda to leave. Benny told Janice he would pay
for Rhonda's ticket to fly back home. Janice said, "No, she could
stay as long as she likes to." Benny slapped Janice, and she started
hitting Benny back. The fighting got out of control. Rhonda told
me to call the police. I told Rhonda I was scared, and Janice always
went back no matter what happened. Rhonda called the police. The
police already knew about my family because the neighbors would
call the police. And they had been to our home on other occasions.
Whenever they came, it was always six or more cops because Benny
was a big man. When they got there, Rhonda and I were on the
porch. Rhonda was flagging them down. When the police came in
the house, Janice and Benny were on the stairs fighting. The police
immediately broke them up. The police told Benny to come outside
and talk to them. Benny refused to go.

Benny said, "This is my house, and I'm not going anywhere."
The police told Benny to put his hands behind his back. Benny
refused, so they pulled their guns out on him.

Rhonda was screaming, "Shoot him!"

Janice screamed, "Please don't shoot him!" Janice said she will
leave the house, so the police put their guns up, and we all got in
Janice's car and left. The police stayed behind with Benny at the
house. Janice took us to a hotel down the street from the house.
Rhonda asked Janice why she didn't let the police kill Benny. Janice
said she didn't want him dead; he was her husband and the father of
Belinda and Benny Jr.

Rhonda told Janice, "If you stay with him, you will end up
dead." I didn't say anything about the situation.

Our hotel room had two beds in it, with a couch. I just lay
on the couch and listened to Janice and Rhonda talk. Rhonda said
she was going to catch a bus back to Texas as soon as she found out
when the next one was leaving. After everyone fell asleep, I began
talking to God silently. I said to God, *I wanted the police to kill
Benny just as bad as Rhonda did, but not in Belinda or Benny Jr.'s
face. That would hurt them for the rest of their life. I still want to kill
him. I'm going to do it in a way I hope no one would find out I did it.
Everything happened so fast tonight. I'm thinking about it, and I don't*

know how to talk to you about it. I know it's wrong to kill someone, but I don't think it's fair that he can hurt me and get away with it. Then I said the Lord's Prayer and told God I love him, and I fell asleep thinking about my deceased mom.

Chapter 22

Morning came. We left the hotel and went home. When we got there, Benny was gone. Janice told us to pack our clothes. We were going to Texas to live. Rhonda went in my room to get her and her baby's stuff, ready to go. All of Rhonda's stuff were gone. When I went to pack my clothes, they were gone too. Janice's, Belinda's, and Benny Jr.'s clothes were gone also.

Janice said, "I know Benny has them."

Rhonda said, "I'm not leaving without my stuff."

Janice told Rhonda, "The only thing we could do is wait till Benny comes home." Janice called Benny's job and found out he's at work. Janice said Benny did that so she can't leave him. Rhonda began getting angry with Janice, using cuss words, telling her it's all her fault. Janice told Rhonda she wasn't going to keep talking to her like that, and she had to wait till Benny came home. I went to Belinda's room and lay across the bed and started talking to God. *Thank you, God, for protecting us last night; and I see you protected Benny too, because the police could have killed him. First, I don't understand why you would let an evil man live, but I figure you didn't want Belinda and Benny Jr. to see that, or maybe you didn't want any of us to see that. Overall, I thank you. I don't mind Rhonda being mean to me, but I don't like it when she's mean to Janice. Could you please soften Rhonda's heart so she won't be so mean to Janice? Please give Janice the strength to move on and away from Benny. Janice can make a better life for all of us. I'm tired of all the pain I have to go through every day. Please hear my cry.* I said the Lord's Prayer and went in the den and started watching TV.

Benny came home. Rhonda went straight to Benny and asked him, "Where is my stuff?" Benny told Rhonda to get out of his face, and he continued to his bedroom where Janice was. Rhonda followed Benny. Once he got in his room, he shut the door in Rhonda's face. When he came out, he went to the attic and gave Rhonda her stuff, then Benny brought all of our stuff down. Our clothes were in trash bags. Benny told me to put everyone's clothes back up, and Janice will take care of her own. Rhonda told Janice to take her to the bus station in the morning. Her ticket was paid for. Janice said okay.

I admired Rhonda so much. She carried herself like a grown person, and it seemed like she had life already figured out. After I put everyone's clothes up, I started playing with Rhonda's baby. I went upstairs to get some water, and Benny and Janice were on the couch hugging and kissing like nothing happened last night. I was so lost for words. Well, later that night while lying in Belinda's bed, I started talking to God. I said, *God, please watch over Rhonda and her baby. Make sure they get home safe and always protect them. Please continue protecting Janice from Benny. I'm still scared he's going to continue hurting her. Give Janice the strength to move on. For me, God, please protect me from Benny. Please get me out of this situation.* I said the Lord's Prayer and told God I love him, and then I went to sleep.

The next morning, I was helping Rhonda get her stuff together. Then we took her to the bus station. I hated to see her and my niece leave, but I knew it's for the best. I was back once again worrying if Benny was going to start coming in my room again. Spring break was over. We were back in school. Life went on like always. Benny and Janice were arguing and fussing again. Benny hadn't been in my room for over a month now.

At least I thought he wasn't coming in my room. One night I was woken up by a nightmare. When I opened my eyes, Benny was standing by my bed playing with himself. At first I thought I was still dreaming until I jumped up, and Benny slung me down on my bed. Benny put his private up and ran back upstairs. I don't know if Janice was awake, but I saw a light on upstairs. I said, *Thank you,*

God, thank you for not letting Benny hurt me. I guess Benny has still been coming in my room. I just didn't know it. I stayed awake after that. It wasn't long before daylight came. I woke Belinda up so we could get ready for school.

Chapter 23

Weeks went by, and it was a Saturday morning. Janice received a phone call from Rhonda. Rhonda told Janice her grandmother had died. Janice told Rhonda we will be there for the funeral. When Janice got off the phone with Rhonda, she told me the funeral will be next Saturday. After Janice said that, I went in my room and said a prayer to God for Rhonda. In the process of me praying, I started crying. It made me think about when my mom died. I missed her so much. I knew how Rhonda felt. The pain never goes away. I was glad we were going to Texas to be with Rhonda.

I was older now, and I understood death a lot better. After I finished praying, I went in the den and started watching TV. I could hear Benny and Janice arguing about he didn't want to go to Rhonda's grandmother's funeral, and he didn't want Janice to go either. So I got up and went to the backyard and sat on our patio so I wouldn't have to hear their argument. Later that evening, we were all eating dinner at the table. Janice told us we were leaving early Friday morning. We're driving to Texas to go to Rhonda's grandmother's funeral. I guess they reached an agreement. Some days passed, and it's about 3:00 a.m. Friday morning. We're up getting ready to head to Texas. When I entered the car, I sat behind Janice purposely, hoping Benny wouldn't say anything.

Before Benny entered the car, he stuck his head in the car and said, "Tammy, you know the routine," so I climbed over Belinda and Benny Jr. and sat down behind Benny. In my mind, I was praying Janice would say something to Benny. But she didn't. I guess she's scared or trying to keep the peace. I just looked out of the window the whole time.

We finally made it to Jefferson, Texas. Benny stopped at a hotel for the night. The next morning, we started getting ready for the funeral. Before we went to the funeral, we went to see Rhonda. It looked like the whole family was there. I got a chance to meet her dad and some of her other relatives. Janice told us to get in the car; it was almost time for the funeral to start. When we arrived at the church, I broke down and started crying again. All I could think about was my mom. Janice grabbed me and said, "It's going to be okay."

Benny told me, "Shut the hell up. That happened about five years ago. You should be over it." I didn't say anything. I just tried to stop crying. Janice told Benny to leave me alone. I asked Janice if I could stay in the car. Janice told me yes, and Benny said hell no. Janice told Benny to leave me alone. Benny decided he wanted to stay in the car with me. I told Janice I changed my mind. I wanted to go inside the church with her. Benny decided to go in with us also. As we walked into the church, I asked God to please help me be strong and not cry.

As soon as we sat down, it sounded like I could hear my mother's voice. She was saying, "Tammy, I'm still here, and I need you to be my big girl right now. It's going to be okay." I don't know if my mind was playing tricks on me, but I felt stronger and felt a sense of joy. I was able to make it through the funeral without crying. After the funeral, we went back to Rhonda's house and waited for her to come back from the cemetery. Rhonda's grandfather and a family member were there also. Her grandfather wasn't well enough to attend the funeral.

Once Rhonda got home, Janice told her we were going back to Colorado because they had to be at work Monday. Rhonda walked us to the car. I asked Rhonda if I could live with her. Rhonda said yes. I asked Janice if I could stay. Janice said yes. Before I could ask Benny to open the trunk to get my suitcase out, he said, "Hell no, she can't stay." He told me to get my ass in the car. I told Janice I needed to use the bathroom, so I went back in the house. I ran out of the back door, and I kept running. I ran up on this park. It had a lot of trees, so I climbed up as far as I could get.

I was up pretty high. I could see the street I ran down, then I saw our car. I knew they were looking for me. Janice even got out of the car and screamed my name. I just sat there holding on to the tree. It started getting dark, so I knew I had to go back. As I got closer to Rhonda's house, I didn't see our car. Once I got in the yard, Rhonda came out and said, "Tammy, where were you? We looked everywhere for you. Janice and Benny left you. I tried to get your suitcase, but Benny wouldn't let me have it. I have some clothes you can wear. My aunt can enroll you in school." Then Rhonda said, "Come inside so I can show you your room, and there is plenty of food left if you're hungry." Rhonda left me in my new room and went to check on her baby. I stood there for a minute. I believe I was in shock. I got down on my knees to pray. While praying, tears were rolling down my face. This time they were tears of joy. I said to God, *Thank you! I'm finally free from Benny; and please, God, take care of Janice, Belinda, and Benny Jr.* I said the Lord's Prayer and went and got something to eat.

After I ate, I went back in my room. My bed was twice the size of my old bed. I had a beautiful dresser with a mirror. The only time I would look at myself in a mirror, it would be a quick glance. People had called me ugly so much that I did not like looking at my ugly face. But as I stood here looking in the mirror, I was feeling different about myself. I was actually getting comfortable with looking at myself, then I lay across the bed and started talking to God. I said, *God, I did all that worrying trying to figure out a way to run a way, and you had it already planned out. I'm not hungry, I got a roof over my head, and most of all, I'm safe for the first time since my mom passed. I'm relaxed. I feel like someone picked me up and placed me here at Rhonda's house. God, I felt like my mom was sitting in church with me today. I understand what she means now when she says she will always be in my heart, and, Mommy, if you can hear me now, thank you for the help today, and I love you with all my heart and soul.*

Rhonda walked in my room. She brought me some of her clothes and shoes I could wear. I said to Rhonda, "Thank you for the clothes and shoes, but most of all, thank you for letting me live here." Rhonda said she was glad I was there, and everything will be fine.

Rhonda said, "I put you some towels out so you can take a bath." After Rhonda left my room, I took a tour of my new home. We had four bedrooms, den, living room, kitchen, and one bathroom. I saw some metal boxes in every room except the kitchen. I went and asked Rhonda what were they. She started laughing and said those were gas heaters. Rhonda said, "When it gets cold, I will show you how they work."

Then I asked Rhonda, "How do you keep the house cool?"

Rhonda said, "Right now the temperature outside is perfect." She pulled back one of the curtains in the living room and showed me an air conditioner in the window and said, "This keeps the house cool, and we also use fans." Rhonda started laughing again and asked me if I had any more questions about the house. I said no and went and took my bath and got in my bed. I was so tired. I said the Lord's Prayer and went to sleep.

Chapter 24

Before day rise, I was woken up by a rooster, singing cock-a-doodle-doo! I looked out of the window, and I saw a rooster standing on top of a little house next door.

I'd seen roosters on TV, but never in someone's backyard. I got dressed and went outside and looked in the neighbor's backyard. She had a lot of chickens, two horses, and two cows. I went and sat on the front porch. The air was so fresh. It seemed like I was breathing better. It was so peaceful. All of a sudden, a flock of chickens came across the front yard. They ran to our neighbor's backyard with the rest of the chickens. The whole animal situation was shocking to me. It was kinda funny to me having farm animals in the neighborhood. I decided to walk around the neighborhood. I couldn't find any sidewalks, so I had to walk on the streets. I didn't walk very long. I went back home in case Rhonda woke up and I wasn't there. As I got closer to our home, I could smell bacon cooking. Rhonda was cooking breakfast. I was like wow! Rhonda was very grown up. I was thirteen, and she was fourteen. Rhonda knew how to take care of herself and her baby. While we were eating breakfast, I asked Rhonda how she learned to do grown-up things. Rhonda said her grandmother taught her how to cook, drive, clean up, pay bills, and, most of all, take care of her baby.

Rhonda told me to help keep the house clean, do laundry, and help her take care of the yard front and back. I told Rhonda that was no problem. I was used to doing those things. I was so happy to be here. Rhonda said her aunt will be over today to help her with her grandfather, and she will ask her if she can enroll me in school

Monday. I said okay and started cleaning up the kitchen and anything else she needed me to do. After I was done, I went and sat on the front porch. Even though I wasn't in the house with Benny, I still thought about all the awful things he had done to me.

And I still wanted to kill him. I figured when I turned eighteen, I'll get a job, buy a car and a gun, and go to Colorado and kill him. Go back to Texas like nothing ever happened. For now I was going to do whatever Rhonda wanted me to do to take care of our home. A lot of Rhonda's family came to visit Rhonda and her grandfather today. Rhonda's house was the family home, so family members were always around. Rhonda's aunt Mary came to me and told me to be ready in the morning; she's going to enroll me in school. I told Aunt Mary thank you, and I will be ready.

I was overwhelmed with emotions inside. I had never been around so many kind people. One of Rhonda's aunts, May, told me I was cute. I smiled and told her thank you. I didn't believe her. I just thought she wanted me to feel welcomed. But it did make me feel good inside. Aunt May sat down beside me and asked me what I wanted to do when I graduate from high school. I said I hadn't decided yet. Aunt May said she's in college right now, and when I graduate, she will help me get into a college. I told her thank you, and I went and sat outside in one of the lawn chairs in the front yard.

As I sat there, I thought about what Aunt May asked me. I never thought about graduating from high school. The only thing I ever thought about was Benny and everything he did to me. I wasn't used to people talking to me. I thought Rhonda's family thought I was slow because I couldn't relate to some of the things they talked about. I felt my conversation wasn't on the level of my age, but everyone was nice anyway. The day went by fast. That night while lying in my bed, I thought about going to school tomorrow. I was nervous about how they were going to treat me.

I started talking to God. I thanked him again for getting me away from Benny and asked him, *Please continue to take care of Janice, Belinda, and Benny Jr. Also, God, I have a new family now, and could you please take care of them also?* I said the Lord's Prayer and went to sleep. Sometime that morning, I was woken up from a nightmare.

I dreamed Benny was in my room. I was fighting him, trying to get away. I thought I was in my old bedroom until I heard the rooster singing, and I realized where I was at. I stayed awake and got ready for school. I also helped Rhonda with her baby.

Rhonda told me the clothes she gave me fit me good, and she had some more clothes to give me. Since she had the baby, they didn't fit her anymore. I told Rhonda thank you again. Rhonda said she was going to school with me and her aunt to help with filling out the paperwork and make sure I get on the right bus. After they left, someone from the office took me to my class. When I entered the class, the teacher had me to introduce myself and told me where my desk was. When I sat down, I could hear the other students saying I talked funny, but no one called me ugly. That made me feel good.

I was surprised to see a mixture of different nationalities, and everyone got along good. All the schoolwork was very easy. I had done most of all the assignments last year in Colorado. Overall, school was great. I didn't have to fight anyone. I figured all the praying I had done, God had answered my prayers, and I was very thankful my homelife was good.

Chapter 25

After living in Jefferson for a couple of months, Rhonda's grandfather died. It seemed like when he died, the joy I felt in his home left too.

I had started smiling and laughing a lot. I thought that was a good thing, until one morning Rhonda asked me why I smiled so much. I said because I was happy. Rhonda said to me, "There is nothing in life to be so happy about every day." I didn't know how to accept that, and I wasn't going to be mean or argue with Rhonda about anything. I was so grateful to be living with her. As time went by, I tried real hard not to smile around her, but I couldn't stop. Even if I was sick or having a bad day, I would still smile. I didn't remember smiling like this when I was in Colorado, or maybe I did, and no one brought it to my attention.

What Rhonda didn't know was even though I smiled, deep down inside me I was crying. The pain and misery I went through in Colorado haunted me every day. One night while lying in bed, I was talking to God. I asked God, *Please take away any pain Rhonda has. I don't understand what is going on with her. She has changed a lot. Whatever it is, please bring sunshine to her life.* I said the Lord's Prayer and fell asleep thinking about how God had blessed me. The year had passed, and my birthday was coming up. Rhonda's birthday was in the same month as mine. One day Rhonda asked me what I wanted to do for my birthday. I said I didn't know.

Rhonda said, "Since our birthdays are in the same month, we should celebrate it together." I told Rhonda that would be nice, and we could do whatever she wanted to do. Rhonda didn't know that to me, my birthday or holidays were just another day to me. I was happy about the fact that Rhonda was concerned and wanted my birthday to be special. Rhonda decided to celebrate our birthdays on my birthday. She bought a beautiful cake with both of our names on it. I felt that was the best thing that ever happened to me in my life, to see my name on that birthday cake.

It's my fourteenth birthday, and I felt so special. Rhonda invited friends and family over. They all came with gifts for both of us. Rhonda also cooked us an awesome birthday dinner. After everyone ate, they sang happy birthday to us. I was like wow! I was on top of the world. I guess I was acting like a little child because Rhonda said, "Tammy, stop acting so silly. You act like you're not used to anything." So I stopped and chilled and kept my excitement inside. Later that night, after everyone left, I told Rhonda thank you for the birthday party. I had a great time. Rhonda said, "You're welcome."

Before I went to sleep, I had my talk with God. I said, *Thank you, God, for blessing me to see another birthday. I never thought I would live this long. I'm truly grateful for the people you have put in my life.* I got on my knees and said the Lord's Prayer and went to sleep.

Chapter 26

Some time went by, and track season had started. I decided to try out. We had to wear a certain type of shorts and shirts for practice. I practiced in shorts and a T-shirt that Rhonda had given me. The coach would tell me every day if I didn't wear the right practice clothes, I couldn't be on the team.

One day the coach came up to me and said if I didn't wear the right uniform, I couldn't be on the team. So that was my last day. I wasn't going to ask Rhonda to buy it for me because she had to take care of her baby. When the weekend came, I decided to walk around the neighborhood, asking people if I could cut their grass or rake their leaves up. It paid off because a lot of people hired me to take care of their yard. Now I was able to help Rhonda with food and bills. Maybe that was why she wasn't happy because she was doing everything by herself. Since I'd been helping Rhonda, she'd been a lot nicer to me. One day I was raking our front yard. I was talking to God like I always did. I was thanking him for making my life better. I had my head down raking, and I heard a voice. Someone said, "How are you doing?" I raised my head up, and a boy was standing in front of me. He said his name was Richard and asked me where Rhonda was. I asked him how he knew Rhonda.

He said, "She is my classmate." Richard said, "You must be Tammy, Rhonda's sister. I live down the street. I'm just passing through headed home. Rhonda told me she had a sister living with her now."

I didn't say much to him. So Richard went on about his business, walking down the road. Sometimes I would be sitting on our front porch steps, and Richard would stop by and try to have a conversation with me. I didn't talk much because I really didn't know how to talk to boys. Our house was a very long house. My sister slept in the back of the house, and I slept in the front of the house. One night I was in bed, and I heard someone moving around in the house. I thought it was Rhonda, so I didn't think anything of it. All of a sudden, there was this man in my room. The more I looked at him, the more I realized it was Richard. He had a knife in his hand. Richard said if I screamed or fought, he was going to kill Rhonda and her baby. He tore my panties off and kept the knife close to my face. I didn't say anything. I just let him rape me. After he was done, he went out of the front door. I locked the door and went and checked on Rhonda and my niece; they were sound asleep. We had three doors in the house that led to the outside. The one in the den was unlocked. I locked it and went in the bathroom and cleaned up. My whole body hurt, and my inner thighs were bruised really bad. I went in my room and got on my knees and started talking to God. I asked God to forgive me if I'd done something wrong.

Cece told me when bad things happen to me, it's because I've been bad. I don't know what I did wrong, but I will do my best to be good. God, please protect myself, Rhonda, and my niece from Richard. I'm really scared of him, and I feel he's been in this house before. He knew his way around. I said the Lord's Prayer and just lay there. I didn't feel like talking anymore. Tears rolled down my face. I thought I was safe here, but I was not safe anywhere. I wasn't going to tell anyone what happened. I didn't want to put that on Rhonda's mind. She had her baby to worry about, and I didn't have anyone else. I only have God.

I thought Benny, Hounddog, and Cece were the only demons running around; but I'd learned they were not the only ones. I'd put Richard on my list to be killed. I was not sure how Richard got in our house, but I was going to be prepared for him next time. He will have to kill me or I will kill him. That morning while I was getting ready for school, Rhonda came in my room. She asked me what's wrong. I said nothing. I had my back to her so she could not see my face, so I couldn't understand why she would think something was wrong.

I continued getting ready for school. While sitting in my class, all I could think about was what happened to me last night.

Rhonda and I lived alone. We couldn't let people know we lived alone. Rhonda said if I told someone, Child Protection Services (CPS) would come and take us away. So I didn't. I couldn't tell the cops or anyone else about what Richard had done to me. After that night, I never saw Richard again. I had nightmares not only about Benny but about Richard too. I had changed back to my old self. I just put on a fake face like I was happy, but deep inside I just wanted to die so I didn't have to live with the pain every day. But for some reason, God won't let that happen. So I will continue to survive.

My happy days were gone, and I was just waking up every day going through the motion to live to see the day I will make Benny and Richard pay. Rhonda had started back being mean to me again. She said she needed more money from me. So I would do more yards, and I even started cleaning people's home to give Rhonda more money, but she still continued being mean. She would complain about my chores and anything else she could fuss about. I had nowhere else to go. I just sucked it up and did whatever Rhonda wanted me to do.

Chapter 27

It's summertime, and I was able to get on a work program for teen-agers. We worked forty hours a week, so I was able to give Rhonda a lot more money. Plus I still had other jobs to do on the weekend. Rhonda had started back being nice to me again. One night I was lying in bed talking to God. I said to God, *Thank you for protecting me every day. I'm starting to get my happiness back. I'm working harder now, and our home is peaceful. Rhonda has stopped fussing at me every day. She has started letting me hang out with her and her friends.* I said the Lord's Prayer and went to sleep.

A few days went by, and Rhonda asked me if I would like to go to a party with her Friday night. I said yes, then Rhonda said, "Don't be acting silly." I said I wanted to go. In my mind, I thought, *I prob-ably will be silly because I've never been to a teenage party or any party. All I know is to be myself.* Friday came, and Rhonda's boyfriend picked us up and took us to the party. The party was at a community center not too far from our home. I saw a lot of classmates there, and I did a lot of dancing. The party was over at twelve midnight. I started looking for Rhonda.

But Rhonda was nowhere to be found. I waited in the parking lot because they had closed the community center. One of Rhonda's classmates named Billy came up to me and asked me if someone was going to pick me up. I told Billy I was waiting on my sister, Rhonda. Billy said Rhonda left with her boyfriend a long time ago. I was the only person left in the parking lot, so Billy said he would wait with me. After about an hour went by, Billy said he would walk me home.

His house was on the way. I said okay; we left walking. I had been around Billy before, so I didn't have bad feelings about him.

Plus I lived in a neighborhood in Colorado way worse than here. Billy said, "Follow me. I know a shortcut." So I did. Billy took me through a trail with very tall grass. All of a sudden, Billy turned around and threw me on the ground. He had his arm pressing against my throat. I could barely breath. With his other hand, he snatched my pants down and raped me and then took off running. I sat there for a minute. I felt like I was going to pass out. I got it together and started walking home. I was in a lot of pain. I prayed to God to help me make it home the rest of the way. When I got home, Rhonda's boyfriend's car was in the driveway. I went to the front door, and it was unlocked. I could hear my sister's boyfriend snoring. I peeped in her room and saw my sister asleep too. I went in the bathroom and took a bath then went to bed. I didn't go to sleep. I didn't pray to God. I told myself it was my fault because I never should have left with Billy. I really didn't understand why this kept happening to me. I just wanted to die. I stayed awake till morning. Rhonda came in my room and asked me if I wanted some breakfast. I told her no. She didn't ask me how I got home or anything.

After Rhonda and her boyfriend had breakfast, she came back in my room and told me I needed to do the dishes and the laundry. I didn't say anything to her. Rhonda said, "Why you're not smiling today like always?" Then she started laughing. I didn't say anything. I just started doing the dishes. Rhonda reminded me of Cece so much. After I was done with everything, I lay across my bed and said the Lord's Prayer. I made a promise to my mom that I would always pray to God no matter what the situation is. I fell asleep thinking about my mom wishing she were still here.

I didn't sleep long. I was woken up by a nightmare about Benny hurting me. My list of people who had hurt me just kept getting longer. I started crying. *I'm all alone in this world. Why is it so evil to me?* I kept to myself. My body and heart were in so much pain. I got up and washed my face and went and started raking one of my neighbors' yard. After I was done, I went home and sat on the front porch step. Rhonda came outside, and when she looked at me, she saw the bruises on my face and neck where I was fighting Billy. Rhonda asked what happened to me.

I told her I got in a fight last night. Rhonda said, "Looks like they won," and started laughing. I just looked at her. Rhonda went back in the house. As I sat there, I started talking to God. I asked God, *Why is my life like this? What do I need to do to make it better? I say I want to die, but deep inside that's not what I want. I just want a normal life.*

Chapter 28

Well, summertime passed, and school was starting back. I knew Rhonda will start back being mean to me because the work program was over. I was going to try to find an after-school job so I can continue to help her.

I was going to the ninth grade this year. That meant I was going to a different school, and it's a walking distance from my home. I was glad to be changing schools. When I was at the eighth-grade school, you had to say "Yes, ma'am" or "Yes, sir," and I would always forget and get sent to detention. My mom never made me say that, and in Colorado, the teachers never made us say it. Benny and Janice didn't make us say that either. It was something new for me. When school started, Rhonda's classmate would give her a ride to school. He told her he could drop me off at school because he had to drop off his cousin at the same school I went to. His name was Ronnie, and we all rode to school together every day, and he would pick us up also. I enjoyed going to this school. I even made some new friends. About a month passed, and I was sitting down on the school steps waiting for Ronnie to give us a ride home like always; only my classmate Kenny hadn't come out of the school yet. Ronnie pulled up. Rhonda wasn't in the car. I asked Ronnie were Rhonda was. He said she had to stay after school. I told Ronnie we had to wait for Kenny. Ronnie said Kenny went home sick earlier. Then he said, "Come on, Tammy, let's go. Rhonda told me to take you home." So I got in the car.

Ronnie was driving faster than he normally did. Ronnie passed my street. I said, "Ronnie, you passed my street." Ronnie said he had to make a quick stop, and he will take me home after that. I said, "Why can't you drop me off first?" Ronnie said it won't take very long. I wanted to jump out of the car, but he was driving too fast. Ronnie pulled into a park. It's the same park I was in when I was hiding from Benny and Janice. I tried to jump out of the car. Ronnie put his arm around my neck. My back was facing Ronnie. He pulled me closer to him. I turned around, and I tried to push his eyes out. He grabbed my hands and hit me in the face and then tried to rip my pants off. I was fighting with everything I had, including kicking. I noticed his penis was hanging out of his pants. I hit it, and he grabbed it and bent over like he was hurt. As I was getting out of the car, he kicked me in my back, and I fell on the ground. Ronnie drove off. I got up and started walking home. My pants were ripped, so I had to hold them together. As I was walking home, a car pulled up beside me; it was Ronnie. He threw my schoolbooks at me and kept going.

I picked my books up and headed home. As I was walking, I thanked God for giving me the strength to fight Ronnie. *I'm asking you, God, to keep giving me the strength to fight.* As I got closer to my house, I was hoping Rhonda wasn't there. I looked a mess. My hair was all over my head, and my pants were ripped. Once I walked in, Rhonda wasn't there, so I took a bath and put some more clothes on. When I looked in the mirror, my lips were busted, and one of my eyes was swelling up. I put some ice on my lip and my eye and just sat on my bed. My back and my jaw were hurting too.

It wasn't long after that Rhonda came home. She came in my room and said she got us a pizza for dinner. Then she said, "What happened to you?" I told her I got in another fight at school. Rhonda said, "Damn, you already ugly enough," and started laughing. At that point, I wanted to jump up and slap Rhonda, but I couldn't because I had to live here, and if she put me out, where will I go? I told Rhonda I wasn't hungry. I spent the rest of the day in my room looking out of my window and talking to God.

The next morning, Rhonda came in my room and asked me if I was going to school. I had a black eye, and my lips were looking pretty ugly. I said, "Yes, I'm going." Then Rhonda said I had to walk because Ronnie called last night and said he could no longer take us to school. I said okay. I was going to walk anyway. I'd gone to school in Colorado with a busted lip and a black eye before. It wasn't a big deal to me. I wanted to tell Rhonda what happened, but she always thought bad of me, and she treated me like I was so dumb. I will keep my problems to myself and live to see another day.

Chapter 29

As I was walking to school, I ran into Kenny. Kenny said, "I was on my way to get you so we can walk to school together. Ronnie called me and said he couldn't pick us up anymore." Kenny said, "What happened to your face?" I told Kenny I got in a fight. Kenny said, "At school?"

I said, "No, and I really don't want to talk about it." Kenny said okay, and we headed to school. I got a lot of looks and questions about my face. I told everyone I got in a fight. I really didn't care how I looked. I was happy I was able to get away from Ronnie more than anything.

Some time passed, and my birthday was almost here. I will be fifteen. One day Rhonda asked me what I wanted to do for my birthday. I told Rhonda to do whatever she wanted to do. She decided to do the same thing as last year. I didn't feel like celebrating. But I did give Rhonda a gift to show her I appreciated everything she had done for me. I gave her a card with a hundred-dollar bill in it. Rhonda gave me a hug and said thank you. That was the first time she ever hugged me. I was thankful. Maybe Rhonda did have a soft side.

I was starting to like boys, but I figured boys would never like me because I was so ugly. One day one of my classmates asked me to go to the movies with him for his birthday. I was so shocked. No boy had ever asked me to go out with them. I told him I had to ask my mom. He said, "Okay, let me know something tomorrow." I said okay. Rhonda and I made people believe our mom lived with us so no one would know we were raising ourselves. I was so excited. I thought maybe I was not that ugly. When I got home from school, I asked Rhonda if I could go to the movies with my classmate Robert this coming weekend. Rhonda said no. I asked her why not. Rhonda said no, end of discussion. I said okay and went in my room to do my homework. After that, I started playing with my niece. She would always put a smile on my face. I would forget about all the pain I carried with me every day. I called her my little angel from God. Then I took a bath and went to bed. I said the Lord's Prayer and fell asleep talking to God about my day.

Sometime that night, I was woken up by a nightmare. I was dreaming Benny was beating Janice, and I was trying to help her, but for some reason, my body wouldn't move. I was begging Benny to stop, then all of a sudden, I could move, but I woke up. I was soaking wet with sweat. I had to take a bath and change my sheets. So I just stayed awake till it was time to go to school. Besides that, I had to let my mattress air-dry too from the sweat. When I got to school, I told Robert my mom said no, I couldn't go to the movies with him. Robert said, "Okay. I understand."

A couple of months passed by. It was on a Saturday evening. I was walking home from doing my neighbor's yard down the street from my house. I could see a car in our driveway. As I got closer, I realized it was Benny's car. Once I got in our yard, I could hear Janice screaming for help. I ran in the house. Benny and Janice were in Rhonda's room fighting over a shotgun. I immediately started helping Janice. Janice got control of the gun. Benny started begging Janice not to shoot. Janice shot anyway, but the gun jammed.

Janice took the gun and hit Benny with it and took off running out of the house. While Janice was running, she was screaming, "Run, Tammy, run!" First, I took off running, but I stopped before I ran out of the door. Benny was a very tall man, so he had to bend his head down to go through the doorway. When Benny came through the front door, I grabbed the doorknob and caught his head in the door. I didn't know where all that strength came from, but I was able to hold the door with his head stuck. I was pulling the door so hard, blood started running down his face. Benny was begging me to let the door go. Benny started saying, "Tammy, I'm sorry for everything I've done to you. Please let me go. You or Janice will never have to worry about me again."

Benny had a hole in his forehead. Janice said it happened when he was in a war, and a bullet fragment did it. Blood had started coming out of that hole in his forehead. So I pulled the door real hard one more time and took off running down the street.

After I ran so far, I stopped to look behind me. Benny wasn't following me, so I headed back to the house. When I got there, Benny was gone, so I sat down on the front porch step and waited for Janice. Finally Janice showed up. I asked her where she went. Janice said she was hiding in the store down the street from the house. Janice asked me why I didn't run with her. I told Janice what I had done to Benny. Janice told me to stop telling lies, and Benny was a big man. There was no way that happened.

Janice said she was glad he was gone. I asked Janice where Belinda and Benny Jr. were. She said they didn't want to leave their dad, so they were with Cece. I didn't tell anyone else what I did to Benny because Rhonda and Janice would always say I was crazy, because I talked to God so much; and I knew if Janice didn't believe me, no one else would. I would always keep my thoughts and the relationship I have with God to myself. Overall, I was so happy to see Janice. A few minutes later, Rhonda and my niece came home.

Rhonda was happy to see Janice too. Janice said she will be staying with us now. Later that night while lying in bed, I started talking to God. The first thing I said was *Thank you, God, for giving me strength to hold Benny's head in that door. I know it was you. I don't want to kill Benny anymore. I don't have to carry those thoughts about killing Benny either. The nightmares may never go away, and everything Benny did to me I'm sure will always be on my mind. But you did bring me some peace of mind that Benny will never hurt me again. So I want to thank you again.* I said the Lord's Prayer and fell asleep thinking about what all happened that day. I guess I slept pretty good last night. No nightmares, and I slept longer.

It's Sunday morning. Rhonda was in the kitchen cooking breakfast. Janice came in my room and said, "Good morning, Tammy." I said good morning. I was sure I had the biggest smile on my face. I felt happy and safe again. I wasn't sure if Janice had deep love for me, but her presence meant the world to me.

Chapter 30

Well, as time passed, Rhonda and Janice argued a lot. I think it was because Rhonda had always been the head of our house, and now Janice was the head of the house and making decisions for us. Rhonda even told Janice she had never been in her life and told Janice to not start acting like a mom now. I just stayed out of the way and prayed to God to fix this situation and bring us closer together. Rhonda had even started complaining to me about the way I cleaned the house up now. I didn't fuss back with her. I would just redo whatever she would be complaining about. But the reality of it all was Rhonda was complaining about what Janice had cleaned up. I guess Rhonda was used to the way I did things. Once Janice got a job, Rhonda stopped complaining about everything. One evening I was sitting on the front porch step talking to God. I was telling God about how I missed and loved my mom so much, how I wished she were still here. I missed her hugs and kisses. I wished I could smell her; she always smelled good. We had so much fun together.

I told God, *I feel so empty without her. Now that Janice is here with me, do you think I should tell her about the things Benny did to me when I was living in Colorado with her and how Cece locked me up in that room with Hounddog, plus things that have happened to me since I've been in Texas?* All of a sudden, I could hear Janice and Rhonda arguing. I told God I will talk to him later that night, and I went in the house to see what was going on. By time I got there, they had stopped arguing.

So I went in the den and started watching TV, and I decided to keep my secrets to myself. Months passed, and school was out for the summer. I started back working for that same summer work program, but I had stopped doing chores for people in the neighborhood, because Janice was helping out with the bills too. The summer flew by. I was now going to the high school with Rhonda. I sure hoped Rhonda was not starting fights at school like she did in Colorado. I rode to school with Rhonda and her cousin.

I walked home from school because Rhonda and her cousin got out of school before I did. One day my teacher asked me to take some papers to the office. When I walked in the office, I saw Richard sitting in a chair. My heart started beating really fast. I gave the office lady the papers and headed for the door. When I reached for the doorknob, two police officers were walking into the office. They put handcuffs on Richard and took him out of the school. Later, I learned he had raped his ten-year-old cousin. I was glad he went to jail. There's no telling how many girls he'd raped. I slept in the same bed Richard raped me in, so the thought of Richard was always on my mind. Just like I slept in the same bed Benny would hurt me in every night. I would always suck it up and live for another day. Later that night while in bed, I said, *God, thank you for putting Richard in jail today. I know it was you showing me that I don't have to worry about him hurting me anymore, or me killing him.* I said the Lord's Prayer and told God I love him and went to sleep.

Chapter 31

The following Saturday, I was sitting in the living room listening to some music. I heard someone knocking on the screen door. The front door was open, and the screen door was locked. I went to the screen door. As soon as I got there, one man asked me, "Do you know Tammy Anderson?"

I said, "Who's asking?"

The man said, "I'm Bobby Anderson, her father."

I said, "Give me a minute." I ran in the den where Janice was. I told her, "There is a man at the front door claiming to be my father. He said his name is Bobby Anderson."

Janice said, "Yes, that's your daddy," and I followed her to the front door. When my mom saw him, she opened the front door and gave him a big hug. She hugged the other man too. Janice said to me, "This is your father, Bobby, and your cousin, Ralph." I said hi. I think I was in shock because I didn't even know what to say. I never even thought about my real daddy, and Janice never told me about him. We all sat down and began talking. I asked Bobby where he had been and why I'd never seen him before now.

Bobby said he and Janice were very young when they got married. Bobby said he worked a lot and left Janice home alone. Then Janice said she moved back home with her father, and Bobby stopped coming around. She met Benny and divorced my father. Janice said she and Benny got married and moved to Colorado. I was already living with her brother, Ray. Bobby thought I was living in Colorado the whole time. Bobby said he and Benny never got along, so he stayed away to keep the peace.

Then I asked Bobby, "How did you find me here?"

Then Ralph, my cousin, said, "I saw your mom at the store one day, and you were with her, so when I got home, I called your father and told him you were living here."

Janice said, "Yes, that's what happened." I said okay, but in my mind I was saying, *I wouldn't let anyone stop me from seeing my kid.* Then Bobby asked Janice if he could talk to her alone. Janice said yes and took Bobby to her room. I just sat there with Ralph. He told me all kinds of stories about Bobby and Janice growing up. I just listened.

About an hour later, Bobby and Janice came back in the living room. Bobby said he had to leave, and he would be back soon to take me to meet his family. I hugged him, and they left. I asked Janice why she never told me about him. Janice said she never thought she would see him again. I didn't ask any more questions. I was just happy to know I had a father, and I thought he cared about me. Bobby also gave me his phone number and said I could call him anytime. Later that day, when Rhonda came home, I told her I met my dad.

Rhonda said she was happy for me. I asked her if it would be okay to call my dad sometimes. Rhonda said only if I called collect. I said okay. That night while lying in bed, I started talking to God. I said, *God, thank you for bringing my dad in my life. I figure sooner or later, my dad will want me to live with him so he can get to know me and I will get to know him.* I said the Lord's Prayer and went to sleep. Well, that night, I had a dream about Benny. I was fighting him so hard I fell out of the bed, and I woke up. I got my tablet out and started drawing different types of designs. When I was younger and living in Colorado with Benny and Janice, I would draw pictures of Benny all the time. I couldn't understand at the time why I would draw pictures of someone I hated, until I saw a story on TV about abused kids. The kids were drawing pictures of their abusers, and the families thought it was just a drawing, but really, the kids were telling them what was really going on because they didn't know how to tell their family or they were scared to tell. That sounded like my story. After that day, I met my dad.

He would visit three or four times a month. But not to see me, only to see Janice. One time I came home from school, and Bobby was there. Bobby and Janice were sitting in our living room talking. I thought Bobby was waiting for me to come home from school to spend some time with me. When I walked in, Bobby gave me a hug and said, "I will see you next time."

As time passed, I saw him less, maybe every three months. One day I decided to call him and ask him if I could spend the weekend with him. When he accepted my call, he immediately started fussing at me about calling him collect and told me, "Don't ever do that again." Bobby said, "What do you want?" in a mean voice. I asked him if I could spend the weekend with him. Bobby said, "Let me talk to Janice."

I told Bobby, "Janice is not here."

Bobby said, "I will call you back later," and hung up the phone. After that, I figured I really wasn't his child, because he just met me, and he wasn't interested in anything about me. I went in my room. My feelings were so hurt. Tears rolled down my face. I really thought Bobby was going to be my savior as well as my protector.

I told God, *I don't understand what is wrong with me. What is so hard about loving me? Maybe it's because I'm so ugly. I was hoping Bobby and I could have a great relationship, and I could tell him about the things that have happened to me, and he would say, "You won't ever have to worry about any of those things happening to you again. I love you, and I will take care of you." Wishful thinking on my part.* I said the Lord's Prayer. I took a bath and went to bed.

Chapter 32

One day I was walking home from school, and a Mexican man pulled up beside me in his car. The man said, "Get in the car. I will give you a ride home." I said no. He pulled the car in front of me and blocked my way. I turned the other way and took off running. He turned his car around and blocked my way again. I turned and ran in the back of someone's house. I cut through some other backyards, so I thought I had lost him. As soon as I got back on the streets, I saw him coming directly toward me. I turned back in someone's backyard and hid behind a shed for a little while, then I headed home, and I didn't see him anymore.

When I got home, I told Janice and Rhonda what happened. They both started laughing. I told them I was scared to death. I said, "Rhonda, we should call the police. Janice lives here with us now, and we don't have to worry about CPS. I'm sure that man is going to try to get someone else, and what if the next person isn't so lucky?"

Janice said, "I'm glad you're safe, and that is all that matters."

Rhonda said I was telling a lie and told Janice, "Don't believe what comes out of Tammy's mouth." Once again I was alone and on my own. I was just waiting to finish school so I can move away.

Later that night while lying in bed, I had a talk with God like I always did. I said, *Thank you, God, for saving me today. I know it was you that gave me the strength to run as fast as I did. Once again I'm not understanding why these bad things keep happening to me. I feel like I have a target on my back or a sign on my forehead that reads, "Take me and hurt me." I will continue to be strong and fight for another day. Maybe when I get older, I will be able to save someone that is in the same position I'm in, and I will listen and believe their story. I will protect them. I have a reason to want to live now. I feel in my heart someone will need me one day, and I promise you, God, I won't let them down. I love you, God, and thank you for never leaving me.* I said the Lord's Prayer and went to sleep.

Chapter 33

Months went by, and Janice started dating this guy. Every now and then, Janice would let him come to our house. His name was Herman. Well, one Saturday Janice and Rhonda were at work. My niece was with her daddy. I was in my room drawing pictures. Someone knocked on the front door. I pulled the curtain back on the front door.

It was Herman, Janice's boyfriend. I didn't open the door. I just said, "Janice is not here." Herman said Janice sent him there to give me some money. I said no, she didn't.

Herman put a twenty-dollar bill on the door window and said, "Here's the money right here."

I said, "I don't want it," and closed the curtain.

Herman continued knocking on the door and said, "Open the door, Tammy." Then I heard a knock on the back door. I ran to the side door. By the time I got there, he was inside our house. I didn't know if the door was unlocked or not.

Herman grabbed me and pushed me down on the floor. I was fighting as hard as I could. He was stronger than me. He was pulling my shorts and panties down. I was pulling my shorts and panties back up and trying to fight him too. He was using his legs to hold my legs open. I tried to stick him in the eyes, but I couldn't because I was trying to keep my pants on. I didn't know when he pulled his penis out, but I could feel it on my leg. All of sudden, Rhonda's uncle Steve pulled Herman off me. Herman ran out of the door. I pulled my pants up.

Uncle Steve asked me if I was okay. I told him, "Yes. Thank you for saving me." Uncle Steve told me to tell Janice. He asked me not to tell Janice he helped me. I said okay, but I felt I needed him to help me tell Janice. Uncle Steve said he was passing by, and he saw the side door open. When he pulled in the driveway, he heard me screaming, so he came to see what was wrong. Then Uncle Steve left. After Uncle Steve left, I checked to make sure all the doors were locked. I was a nervous wreck.

I went in my room and told God, *Thank you for sending Uncle Steve to help me.* I told God, *I'm starting to not feel safe here anymore. I thought things would be better with Janice here. I'm going to tell Janice what Herman did to me when she gets home.* Well, when Janice got home, I started telling her what happened to me today.

Janice said, "Look how you're dressed. You were asking him to rape you." It's like she didn't hear anything about how he tried to give me money and how he forced himself on me. At that time, my heart dropped to the floor.

I felt like I weighed a ton. I went in the backyard and sat on the back porch. Tears started running down my face. I was shocked Janice would say something like that. I loved Janice so much. I was hoping and praying she loved me the same. I thought she was a better person since Benny wasn't in her life. I sat in the backyard for hours thinking about my life. I was back where I started when I was in Colorado. I was back numb to life again. I was not crying anymore. I was going to continue to fight for my life. I had no choice. I had nowhere to go.

When I went back in the house, Rhonda had made it home, and Janice had left. Rhonda asked me if I was hungry. I told her, "No, I'm okay."

Rhonda said, "You need to eat something. You need to put some meat on those bones." I didn't say anything. I just went in my room and sat there looking out of the window. I wondered if I had told Janice what Benny was doing to me while I was in Colorado, would she have helped me? I never could understand how that went on, and Janice was in the house while Benny was hurting me.

Even though I will never know the truth, it stayed on my mind. After that day, I never saw Herman again.

Chapter 34

Some time went by, and Janice started dating a different guy. This time she got married and moved in with him. His name was Eddie, and they lived on the other side of town, not too far from us. Rhonda and I didn't care for her husband, but that didn't matter; it was her life. We went back to living by ourselves again. I was in junior high school, and Rhonda was a senior. We only had to make one more year and Rhonda will be eighteen, and we wouldn't have to worry about CPS or anyone knowing we lived alone.

Sometimes Janice and her husband would come visit us. There was one particular day Janice and her husband were visiting us. Rhonda wanted to buy a family box of chicken, but she was short two dollars, so she asked Janice for the money. Janice said she didn't have any money. Eddie volunteered to give Rhonda the money, but he said he wanted his money back. Rhonda said, "The next time I see you, I will give it back to you."

Well, every time Janice and Eddie would come over to visit, Eddie would always ask Rhonda for his money. Rhonda would always say she didn't have it. I think Rhonda thought it wasn't a big deal; it was only two dollars. I felt the same way. Eddie would always talk crazy to everyone around him, and Rhonda and I thought he was mentally crazy for real, but he wasn't our problem.

One Sunday evening, Rhonda and I were watching a movie on TV. Janice and Eddie came over. Janice sat down, but Eddie didn't. Eddie asked Rhonda for his money. Rhonda said she didn't have it. I told Eddie, "I got it. Let me go get it for you."

Eddie said, "No, I want it from Rhonda."

Rhonda and Janice started laughing at Eddie. Janice told Eddie it was only two dollars. "Stop talking about it. Tammy said she would give it to you."

Eddie's voice got louder and told Rhonda, "This is the last time I'm going to ask for my money." Rhonda and Janice started laughing again. Eddie said, "Oh, y'all think it's funny." He pulled out his gun and pointed at Rhonda. Rhonda's daughter was sitting on her lap.

I asked Eddie to put the gun away. "Please don't shoot Rhonda. She has her baby, and her baby needs her."

Eddie said he didn't give a damn. "Rhonda thinks I'm playing about my money." I told Janice to talk to Eddie. Janice kept laughing and said Eddie wasn't going to do anything. I was like what the hell was wrong with Janice? You don't play with guns like that. I looked at Rhonda. Tears were rolling down her face.

I got in front of Rhonda and told Eddie, "If you want to shoot somebody, shoot me." Eddie told me to move out of the way. I told Eddie, "No, and please put the gun up."

Eddie said, "Tammy, you don't have anything to do with this. Move."

I told Eddie, "I'm not moving." Janice was still laughing.

Eddie put the gun down and said, "Rhonda, you're blessed today. Tammy saved you." Eddie told Rhonda, "You can have those two dollars. Now you know I don't play about my money." Eddie went out of the door, and Janice followed him. When I turned around and looked at Rhonda, she was shaking and crying. I tried to get my niece from her, but she didn't want to let her go. Rhonda said if I didn't step in front of her, she believed Eddie really would have shot her. I told her, "I feel the same way. I don't understand why Janice thought that was so funny."

Rhonda continued sitting there. I think she was in shock. Then I went in my room so I could talk to God. I said, *God, thank you for stopping Eddie from shooting Rhonda and her baby. I know you know what was going through my mind at the time. I thought for a second,* Go ahead and shoot me and put me out of my misery. *But I quickly snapped back because just maybe if he had shot me, that means he was going to shoot Rhonda and her baby too.* I said to God, *What kind of mother would sit back and watch her man pull a gun on her daughter and laugh about it even though she thought he was playing? No one plays like that. I'm beginning to think Janice is crazy like her husband. God, thank you for protecting us.* I said the Lord's Prayer.

Then I heard my sister in the kitchen. I asked her if my niece was asleep. She said yes. I asked Rhonda if she was okay. She said yes. I could see in her face that she wasn't. She started cooking dinner. I think cooking was a way she dealt with stress or any problems she would have. Anytime she would be upset about something, I noticed she would cook. I wished I could tell her to pray. Praying for me gave me the strength to get past all the awful things I'd been through. I know in my heart God is here for me. My deceased mom taught me that, and I believe her. She was the only person in the world who loved me.

Rhonda would call me crazy when she would catch me talking to God. So I wasn't going to suggest praying. I will keep my thoughts to myself. I went in the den and started watching TV. Later that evening, Rhonda and her baby went to visit her aunt. I was home alone, and Rhonda very seldom locked the doors, so I got up to make sure all the doors were locked. When I made it to the front door, Rhonda's uncle Steve was standing in the living room. It scared me at first, because I wasn't expecting anyone to be in the house.

Uncle Steve was the husband of Rhonda's aunt Mary, the one she went to visit. Uncle Steve said, "Hi, Tammy! I was passing by and was just checking on you." I said hi. Uncle Steve asked me if I needed anything. I said no. Uncle Steve said, "Here is twenty dollars. Go get yourself something to eat." I took the money and said thank you, and Uncle Steve left. I didn't understand why he did that, but I was appreciative and kept it to myself. After checking all the doors, I went in my room and started drawing pictures of flowers.

Chapter 35

Two weeks went by, and I was in the den watching TV. Rhonda came in the den and said she was going over her aunt's. I said okay. I was waiting on a commercial to come on before I got up to check the doors to make sure they were locked. Before I made it to the front door, Uncle Steve grabbed me from behind and pinned me against the wall, while saying, "I'm not going to hurt you." I had a sundress on. He started feeling on my private area, pulling my panties to the side. I was scared to scream, then he let me go.

Uncle Steve said, "I'm sorry. I don't know why I did that." Then he reached in his pocket and gave me a hundred-dollar bill and said, "Please don't tell anybody." I said I won't, and he left. As soon as he left, I started talking to God. I said, *Thank you, God, for protecting me from Steve. I thought he was going to hurt me, but I guess he changed his mind, or you helped him change his mind. I really thought he was a good guy since he protected me from Herman. But I know I can't trust anyone no matter what. My list of secrets is getting longer. I feel if I was to tell anyone in my family, they wouldn't believe me, or they would say it's my fault, and they would probably put me out on the streets.*

Well, God, I hope you're not disappointed in me. Please forgive me, God, if I have made wrong decisions. I've never had anyone to show me the right way to live or have anyone to tell when someone hurts me. I'm just trying real hard to make it to eighteen and graduate from school and move away. I love you, God, and please continue to protect me. I need you in my life. I went back and started watching TV, but all I could think about was what just happened to me. After that day, every time Rhonda went to her aunt's, I went with her.

Rhonda's aunt was always so nice to me. It made me feel guilty knowing what I knew about her husband, and I knew I was not the only one he's doing that to, I'm sure.

Chapter 36

Some months passed, and Rhonda asked me to go to a graduation party with her. Since it was her graduation party for the seniors, I decided to go. When we got there, Rhonda asked me if I liked the decorations. She was part of the decorating committee. I told Rhonda it was beautiful; they did a great job.

I was having a great time dancing until someone tapped me on the shoulder. I turned around. It was Billy, the guy who raped me when I went to that last party with my sister about three years ago. Rhonda had left me, and Billy walked me home, and he raped me on the way home. I didn't say anything to Billy. I went and sat down at the table and kept my eyes on Rhonda for the rest of the night so she couldn't leave me again. As I sat there, I couldn't believe he came up to me like he hadn't done anything wrong to me. I was so into thinking about that night I lost focus on my sister.

I didn't see her anywhere, so I went outside. Rhonda was getting in the car with someone. I ran to the car and asked her, "Please don't leave me."

Rhonda said, "I will be right back. Go back inside and have fun." I told her my stomach hurt real bad. So she asked her friend if he would take me home. He said sure, and they dropped me off at home and left. I took a bath and went to bed. I said the Lord's Prayer. I fell asleep thinking about what happened to me that night Billy walked me home. Early that morning, I was woken up by my sister. Rhonda said I was screaming and fighting in my sleep, and she came to see what was wrong. Rhonda asked me if I was dreaming someone was trying to hurt me. I said yes. Rhonda said, "Hurt you how?" I said a monster was trying to eat me. Rhonda said, "You need to stop watching scary movies."

I said, "You're right. I will stop." But really, it was another bad dream about Benny hurting me. I went to bed thinking about what Billy had done, but the dream was about Benny. I got up and made my bed up. As soon as the sun came up, I went outside and sat on the front porch steps. As I sat there, I thought about dying. *I feel I will never be in a happy place. I have no purpose in life, and if I'm dead, I won't feel the pain I carry every day. No one will miss me because no one cares.* I couldn't come up with a way to die, and I was tired of thinking about it, so I started raking leaves up on the side of the house into piles.

Rhonda came outside and said she was going to the store and asked me to watch her daughter; she was still asleep. I said okay and went in the house and checked on my niece; she was still asleep. As I was headed to the den, Steve caught me from behind and pinned me up against the wall. This time he didn't pull my pants down. He rubbed his penis against my butt, and I felt something wet on me. He put his penis up and gave me a hundred-dollar bill and left out of the back door. There was a trail behind our house that led to a street. I couldn't figure out how he would know when I was alone. Steve would never rape me. He would rub his penis against me and leave. I was guessing he would be somewhere watching our house. I went and changed clothes because Steve put some wet stuff on me. I thanked God my niece didn't wake up. She talked good, and she could tell her mom.

As soon as I got dressed, Rhonda walked in. I went outside and brought the rest of the groceries in. My niece was still sleeping. Rhonda asked me if I had any money because she spent all her money on groceries. I went in my room to get some money out of the box under my bed, and it was empty. I knew Rhonda had got it. We were the only people in the house. I usually just gave her money. She didn't have to ask, so that was strange to me for her to ask me for money. I was saving money in case I ever had to run away and for when I graduated.

I gave Rhonda the hundred dollars Steve gave me. Rhonda asked me where I got the money. I told her I had saved it up. Rhonda gave me a funny look. She was waiting for me to say something about my money missing. I didn't say anything about the missing money. I put the groceries up and went outside and put the leaves in bags. When I finished that, I went and sat on the porch steps. While sitting there, Steve drove past the house, waving and smiling at me. I didn't smile or wave back.

I started talking to God. I said, *God, if Rhonda would have asked me for money, I would have given it all to her. By her taking it, that lets me know she snoops through my stuff like Benny did. I'm so grateful that she lets me live here. I don't care about the money. I will find a better hiding place. I love Rhonda even though I know she doesn't love me. God, I need you to help me stop Steve from popping up. I'm scared someone is going to catch him hurting me, and because I'm not fighting back nor am I telling anyone, everyone will say it's my fault. I don't have evil feelings toward Steve. I don't know. Is it because he's not rough with me or because he gives me money? Either way, it's all wrong.* After I was done talking to God, I went in the den and started watching TV for the rest of the evening.

Chapter 37

Some months went by. I was home alone, and I had all the doors locked. I heard someone come in. I figured it was Rhonda, but it wasn't. It was Steve. I asked him how he got in the house. He said he had a key to every door. Steve said he and his wife used to live there.

Steve asked me to face the wall, and I had a long T-shirt and panties on. I faced the wall. Steve pulled my T-shirt up and rubbed his penis against my butt. Some wet stuff came out of his penis, then he put his penis up and gave me a hundred dollars and left. I was not scared of Steve. I was scared of getting caught. I knew it would ruin the family if anyone knew. The money helped me a lot. It seemed like Steve would come around when I really needed the money the most. I would give Rhonda half, if not all. Rhonda stopped asking where I got the money and started saying thank you; we needed it.

It made me happy that I could help Rhonda, and she would treat me nicer. I hated when holiday rolled around because all the family would be together. Steve and Mary would be there together, and they seemed like they loved each other so much. I didn't want to mess that up. When I prayed at night, I wouldn't talk about Steve anymore. I would ask God, *Please forgive me for what I'm letting Steve do to me. I know one day I will have to pay for my wrongdoing.* This school year went by so fast. Steve didn't pop up anymore, and I was thankful for that. Summertime was here.

I was working the summertime work program for teenagers at a grocery store at night and weekends. I was saving as much money as I could because after I graduated from high school, I was moving out. I opened up a savings account at the bank so Rhonda can't steal my money. I kept my savings book with me anytime I left home. I knew Rhonda still went through my stuff when I was not home. I can tell when she did because I would leave my things a certain way, and when I got home, they're not the same way I left them.

Summertime passed. I was a senior now. Lord knows I never thought I would make it this far. I really thought I would be dead. Overall, I was glad I made it, and I was almost there. One day I was sitting in class with my classmates. We were talking about having kids and getting married when we finished school. Every one of them wanted kids. One of my classmates asked me how many kids I wanted. I said none. She asked me why. I told her I never thought about that. But deep inside I was thinking, *This world is so evil. Why would I want to bring a child in this world to be mistreated?*

The school bell rang, and it's time to go home. I always walked home with my classmates who lived close to me because I still thought about when that man tried to get me to get in his car. When I got home, I did any chores I needed to do, and I did my homework. Then I lay across the bed and talked to God. As always, I said, *Thank you, God, for protecting me and my family. I've decided I don't want to kill anybody anymore. I've accepted the nightmares because they're not going away, but at least Benny can't hurt me anymore.*

Then I heard a knock on the door. It was my classmate Lisa. Since Rhonda was eighteen, we didn't have to hide anymore. Rhonda let me have company sometimes now. Lisa and I took the chairs off the porch and sat outside in the yard and talked until it was time for her to leave. When I went back inside, Rhonda mentioned our birthdays were coming up and asked what I wanted to do. I told Rhonda I wanted to do whatever she wanted to do. Rhonda said okay. I'd developed a friendship with my classmate Robert. His birthday was in the same month as mine.

A couple of years ago, Robert asked me to go to the movies with him for our birthday. Rhonda said no back then. I was on the phone talking to Robert, and he asked me to go the movies with him. Robert said, "We are older now. Surely your mom will let you go."

I told Robert, "I will ask her. I will let you know when we get to school tomorrow." When I got off the phone, I asked Rhonda if I could go to the movies with Robert this coming weekend. Rhonda said yes.

I told Rhonda thank you, and I went back in my room. I was so excited. I'd never felt this way. I just knew it felt good. I went and washed the dinner dishes and took a bath and went to bed. I started talking to God. I said to God, *Maybe this world isn't so bad after all. My birthday last year was no big deal. I feel this one is going to be special.* I said the Lord's Prayer and went to sleep. When I got to school the next day, I didn't see Robert anywhere. We had different schedules, so that wasn't unusual.

Robert found me after school. He asked me what my mom said. I told Robert she said yes. Robert hugged me. I guess he was excited too. Robert said, "I will call you later," and he told me to check on what movie I wanted to see. I had to walk home alone because all my classmates had already left. I asked God to protect me and help me get home safe. I made it home safe. I thought about that big hug Robert gave me; it made me even more excited. When I got home, Rhonda was in the kitchen cooking. I told Rhonda hello. Rhonda said hello back and said I couldn't go to the movies this weekend because she had made plans for Friday and Saturday, and I needed to babysit. I said okay. I went and called Robert and gave him the bad news. Robert said, "Ask her if you can go Sunday."

I told Robert to hold on. I asked Rhonda if I could go Sunday. Rhonda said yes. I told Robert I could go.

Robert said, "After the movie, we will go get something to eat." I said okay, and we continued talking on the phone till it was time for us to go to bed.

I said the Lord's Prayer and fell asleep. I didn't sleep good that night. A nightmare woke me up. I dreamed Benny was hurting me, and I was trying to get away from him. My sister Belinda was begging him to stop. I fell out of the bed, and that woke me up. My heart was beating so fast. I'd never had a dream with Belinda in it. I started praying to God to protect Belinda. *Please, God, don't let Benny hurt Belinda.* I was having all kinds of thoughts going through my mind after that dream. I couldn't go back to sleep after that. I decided to make Robert a birthday card since I didn't buy him anything for his birthday, and the next day was his birthday. When I got to school, Robert came up to me before school even started.

I said, "Happy birthday, Robert!" and gave him his card. After he read it, he said, "Thank you. I love it." He gave me a big hug. He picked me up off the ground. That made me even more excited because I thought he really liked me. It's Friday, so I will be babysitting my niece tonight. I always loved spending time with her.

Robert called me early Saturday morning and told me happy birthday. He asked me if it would be okay if he brought me a gift today. I told Robert, "No, I can't have boys over." I told Robert he could give it to me Sunday. Robert said okay. I told him I didn't have a gift for him. Robert said, "Yes, you do."

I said, "If I do, what is it?"

Robert said, "You can give it to me Sunday." I didn't have a clue what he was talking about. I just said okay. Robert said, "I've already picked a movie for us. I will pick you up at six o'clock." I said okay and got my day started. Rhonda had made a chocolate cake for our birthday. It was a delicious chocolate cake.

It made me think about how Benny made my cake fall when I was in Colorado. I was so glad I was not there anymore. Rhonda was going out with her boyfriend for her birthday. My niece and I spent the day together. It was the best birthday ever. We danced, played games, and played with her dolls. Later that night, I taught her an easy prayer to say before she went to sleep, the same one my mom taught me when I was little like my niece.

I stayed awake watching TV until Rhonda got home. When Rhonda got home, she said, "Why are you still awake?" I told her I couldn't sleep. I went to bed after that. I was nervous about the next day. I had never gone out with a boy. I fell asleep thinking about Robert. It's Sunday morning, and my sister was up cooking breakfast. It seemed like the day went by so fast. Rhonda took my niece to go visit her father's grandmother, and she told me to enjoy my day. I said thank you, and Rhonda and my niece left.

Chapter 38

Robert was at my house six o'clock on the dot. I came outside before he could knock. Robert said, "Don't you want me to meet your mom?"

I told Robert, "She's asleep. You can meet her another day." Robert was being raised by both of his parents. I told Robert my mom was a single parent. When we got to the car, I went to open the door.

Robert said, "Don't touch that handle. Let me open the door for you." I was like he's a gentleman.

Once we got in the car, Robert gave me a bouquet of roses for my birthday. I was so happy. No one had ever given me flowers. I said thank you and tried to be cool as if I was used to getting flowers. But really, I wanted to scream and act silly. The flowers were beautiful. I had a big smile on my face. When we made it to the movies, Robert said, "Don't touch the door. Let me open it for you."

I was like *Wow! I'm liking this date.* When I got out of the car, Robert grabbed my hand, and we walked into the movie theater.

Robert even put his arm around me while watching the movie. I felt like I was on top of the world. When the movie was over, Robert gave me a smack on the lips. I didn't see it coming, but I played it off. First time for that too. Once we got in the car, Robert asked me if it would be okay if we had pizza for dinner. I said yes. Robert said he had one stop to make before we go eat. Robert drove to a wooded area. No houses around and no streetlights. I asked Robert, "Where are we going?"

Robert said, "You'll see." He pulled in a field surrounded by woods and cut the car off.

I said, "Robert, what are you doing?"

Robert said, "You can give me my birthday present now."

I said, "What are you talking about?"

Robert said, "You. Take your clothes off." I said no. Robert said, "I'll take my clothes off first," and he did.

I said, "I'm not going to take my clothes off. Take me home."

Robert said, "Yes, you are." He tried to take my clothes off. We were fighting.

Robert stopped fighting me and said, "Get out my car."

I said, "No, take me home." I wasn't going to let him leave me out there.

We started fighting again. Robert stopped fighting and started driving in the field real crazy, doing donuts and whatever else he could do. I kept begging him to stop and take me home. He stopped driving crazy and said, "I'm going to take you home after you have sex with me. I'm already naked. All you have to do is take your clothes off." I told him no and we will be fighting all night. Robert took off driving really fast out of the field. Once we got on the street, he tried to push me out of the car while he was driving. I held on to his arm. I was screaming and begging him to take me home. Robert headed toward my house. He was still naked. He was acting like a psycho. Robert said I should be thankful he gave me the time of day, because I was so fucking ugly. I just listened because all I wanted to do was make it home. I thought about jumping out of the car while he was driving, but I was scared I would get run over. Besides that, he was headed in the right direction. When we pulled up in my driveway, he started punching me as I was getting out of the car.

Robert threw my purse at me, and it hit me in the face. He drove off after that. I went in the house. Once I got in, I could hear Rhonda snoring. I went in the bathroom to see how bad my face was. My bottom lip was busted, and one of my eyes was swollen pretty bad. My whole body was hurting. I got some ice and rotated it from my lip to my eye. Then I lay on the bed and thought about what just happened.

I knew I wasn't going to be able to go to school tomorrow. I was hurting pretty bad. I stayed awake all night. That morning when my sister got up, she didn't come in my room. She always left before I got up for school. I stayed home that day. Robert and I had been friends for a long time. I never thought he would have treated me like that or hurt me like he did. I took some Tylenol and kept putting ice on my face all day. Later that day, when Rhonda came home, I was on the couch in the den. Rhonda came in the den. She looked at me and said, "Damn, what happened to you?" I lied and told Rhonda I got in a fight with a boy at school. Rhonda said, "Who was it?"

I told her, "It's this boy named Jerome. Don't worry about it. They suspended him from school."

Rhonda said, "It looks like he hurt you pretty bad." Rhonda asked me, "Do you want to go to the hospital?"

Chapter 39

I told her, "No, I will be okay." Later that night while lying in bed, I started talking to God. I said, *God, I don't understand why this keeps happening to me. I want to thank you, God, for giving me the strength to fight Robert. Thank you, God, for not letting Robert get a chance to hurt me like some people have in my past. I pray one day that I can say thank you for something positive that I have accomplished in life. Please forgive me, God, if I don't have a lot to talk to you about. My body hurts so bad. I just want to lie here.* I said the Lord's Prayer and fell asleep thinking about my deceased mom and how she loved me so much. I missed her so much.

I stayed out of school for a week, to give my body time to heal. I didn't worry so much about how I looked because I was used to black eyes and busted lips. My first day back to school, I didn't see Robert anywhere. My classmates asked me what happened. I told them I got in a fight with a boy last weekend. Everyone wanted to know who the boy was. I told them he wasn't from our school, and he was out of high school. My classmates were so nice to me. They asked me if I needed help with anything. They really made me feel good, that they cared and were concerned about me. I didn't want to bring attention to myself or Rhonda. I asked God to forgive me for lying. I didn't know how to handle the situation. I was used to keeping everything a secret. That evening when I got home, I decided to call my dad and tell him everything I'd been going through. I walked down the street from my house to the neighborhood store and got five dollars' worth of quarters so I could call him on the pay phone. That way he couldn't fuss about me calling him collect. I called my dad, and he answered. I said, "Hi, Dad," and I just broke down and started crying.

My dad said, "Stop crying. Tell me what's wrong, Tammy." I told him what Robert did to me. My dad said, "What you telling me for? What you want me to do about it? What you do to him?"

I said, "Nothing. Forget about it." I hung the phone up. I cried all the way home. I cried all day.

Rhonda said, "Why you crying so much?"

I said, "I don't feel good." But really, my dad hurt my heart.

That night, I said the Lord's Prayer and cried myself to sleep.

Chapter 40

Months passed, and my graduation was almost here. Everyone at school was talking about going to college and what type of job they were going to do when they finished college. One of my classmates asked me what college I will be attending. I said I hadn't decided. In my mind, no one had really talked to me about college. I didn't even understand why people even go to college. I really didn't know anything about life. All I knew was I wanted to work and get my own place.

Later that night, I thought about when my classmate asked me what I was going to do when I graduated. I said to myself, *I know I don't want to be married or have kids. I don't want to go to college because I'm scared I will be fighting boys off me.* One day while sitting in my art class, my teacher called me to his desk. He handed me some papers. He told me he was giving me a scholarship to go to a designing art school. He told me I will do well in that field. He said I was naturally talented. I said thank you and accepted the papers. He said, "Are you excited?" I said yes. He said, "Take the papers home and show them to your parents." I really wasn't excited. I didn't see a reason to be. When I got home, I didn't look at the papers. I threw them in the trash. I didn't have anyone to tell. My counselor would come by the house sometimes wanting to talk to my mom about me going to college. I would always tell her my mom was at work. She would leave papers for my mom to read.

I would always throw the papers in the trash. I couldn't tell her my mom didn't live there. I wasn't going to tell Rhonda about the counselor helping me get into college because Rhonda called me dumb all the time. I was a smart student. I made As and Bs. I signed my own report cards. Rhonda never asked to see my report cards, so she really didn't know how smart I was, nor did she care. I understood her; she wasn't my mother. Months passed, and my graduation was tomorrow night.

I was lying in bed talking to God. I said, *I made it, God, I'm finally graduating. I would have never made it if I didn't have you. I have been through so much to get here.* Tears were running down my face as I talked to God. I could hardly talk to God because I was crying so hard. *I'm wishing my deceased mom could be here to see me. I know it is you, God, that gave me the strength to keep going no matter what. I wanted to give up so many times. Thank you again, God, and I love you.* I said the Lord's Prayer and fell asleep thinking about graduation.

Well, it's graduation day. I was excited and ready to get my diploma. I invited my uncle Ray (Dad), but he didn't come. Janice bought me an outfit, and Bobby bought me some diamond earrings for graduation. I loved the gifts. Bobby said, "Don't lose your earrings. Take good care of them. I paid a lot of money for your earrings." I said okay. Bobby left right after graduation. He said he had to be at work in the morning. We hugged, and he left. I went out partying with my classmates. I had a wonderful time. That morning when I woke up, I still had my earrings on. When I took them off, one of the diamonds was missing from one of the earrings. I felt really bad because that was the only gift my dad had given me. I told Rhonda about it.

Rhonda said, "The box the earrings came in said Zales Jewelry. I will take you to Zales to exchange for another pair."

I told Rhonda I didn't have a receipt; and my father, Bobby, had driven back home to Dallas. Rhonda said they knew their merchandise, and it was worth a try. When we got to the Zales store, I told the salesperson I had got these earrings from my father yesterday for a graduation gift, and a diamond fell out of one of them.

The salesperson said, "Go look on the table in front of the store and get you another pair."

I said, "You're not going to get me another pair out of the jewelry case? My dad said they were expensive."

The salesperson went and got me a pair of earrings off the front table, and she said, "These are the same ones you have." I asked her how much they cost. She flipped the box and showed me the price. It said $19.99. Rhonda fell out laughing. I said, "I don't know what was the point in him telling me they were expensive." The salesperson put them in a bag, and we went home. Rhonda laughed about the earrings all day and told everybody who was around us how cheap my dad was.

I didn't worry about the earrings. I was going to wear them whether they were fake or not. I didn't understand why Bobby felt the need to tell me they were real, and they weren't. I was happy that he came to my graduation, and I was very thankful for the gift. Even though I'd graduated, I still felt lost. I'd watched Rhonda over the years, how she'd taken care of me and my niece. So I knew how to take care of myself. I just didn't know what to do with myself.

Felicia Diane Williams is from a small town called Marshall, Texas. After Felicia finished high school, she attended Draughon Business College majoring in accounting. Later in life, she became a single mom of two. Felicia decided to take her kids and move to Fayetteville, North Carolina, where she attended Fayetteville Technical College. Felicia received a certificate in industrial mechanical engineering. As soon as she graduated from Fayetteville Technical College, she started working for a company called Cutler Hammer in Fayetteville, North Carolina. Felicia stated she liked her job so much her plans were to retire from there. After Felicia had been there for a couple of years, her mother became sick, so Felicia decided to move to Longview, Texas, to take care of her mom. Once her mom was able to take care of herself, she started working for Community Bank. While Felicia was working for Community Bank, she had a terrible car accident that almost cost her, her life. While Felicia was recovering from the accident, her coworkers took time out of their lives to raise money to help Felicia with her bills and keep food on her table. Her coworkers had bake sales, made Christmas stockings to sell, and set up donation jars in stores all over Longview, Texas, for her family. Felicia's customers at the bank even donated money to help her family. Felicia stated she was very grateful and thankful to everyone. She said they all were her angels from God. Once Felicia was well enough, she returned to work. Four years later, Felicia was in another terrible car wreck; only this time it left her disabled and unable to return to work. Still to this day, Felicia doesn't know how her body will react from day to day. She has developed osteoarthritis, and she has permanent nerve damage all over her body. Felicia says sometimes her fingers hurt so bad she can't write, or she shakes so bad she can't keep the pencil still enough to write. It's taken Felicia five years to write this book, *Relationship with God,* and she has decided to share it with the world.